THE WINE GUIDE

HOW TO CHOOSE, SERVE AND ENJOY IT

THE WINE GUIDE

HOW TO CHOOSE, SERVE AND ENJOY IT

AN EXPERT INTRODUCTION FROM GRAPE VARIETIES AND CLASSIC
WINES TO TASTING TECHNIQUES, WITH 160 PHOTOGRAPHS

STUART WALTON

southwater

This edition is published by Southwater
an imprint of Anness Publishing Ltd
Blaby Road, Wigston
Leicestershire LE18 4SE
info@anness.com

www.southwaterbooks.com; www.annesspublishing.com

If you like the images in this book and would like to investigate using them for publishing,
promotions or advertising, please visit our website www.practicalpictures.com for more information.

A CIP catalogue record for this book is available from the British Library.

Publisher: Joanna Lorenz
Senior Editor: Felicity Forster
Designers: Sheila Volpe and Ian Sandom
Cover Design: Jonathan Davison
Picture Researcher: Lynda Marshall
Special Photography and Styling: Steve Baxter with Roisin Neild
Illustrator: Madeleine David
Production Controller: Mai-Ling Collyer

Photographs: All photographic material supplied by Cephas Picture Library, with the following exceptions.
Bridgeman Art Library: 8 (courtesy Pushkin Museum, Moscow), 9 (courtesy British Library, London).
Jane Hughes: 41 (right). Patrick Eager: 50–1. SuperStock: 42, 43 (right), 61 (top).

Previously published as part of a larger volume, *The World Encyclopedia of Wine*

CONTENTS

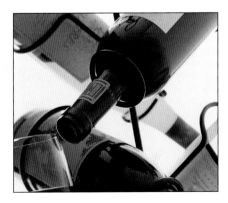

INTRODUCTION

Van Gogh's depiction of grape-harvesting at Arles in the 1880s (above) would still be recognizable today in parts of southern France.

The past century has seen more revolutionary change in the world than any other before it, and the world of wine has been swept right up along with it. At the dawn of the 20th century, wine was just a simple agricultural product, mostly made by the rural populations of a few countries in western Europe, in pretty much the same way they had made it since medieval times. There may have been famous estates, such as the great châteaux of Bordeaux, and there may have been illustrious celebration wines like champagne and vintage port, but what most people drank most of the time was plain old uncomplicated wine – red or white.

By the time the new millennium broke upon us, the global wine industry was a complex edifice of many mansions. Within its walls, different schools of thought contended with each other in sometimes courteous, sometimes embittered battle, as those outside – the loyal consumers of wine – struggled to keep track of it all, while being assailed on all sides by a combination of aggressive marketing and anti-alcohol campaigns. Wine is a hot political issue as never before, as witness the enormous, heartening spread of wine blogging all over the world. We all have opinions about wine, and we're all entitled to express them.

One of the most vigorous debates has been about how wine is made. Nobody can pretend that it isn't nowadays a highly technological process, involving critical decisions at every level, from the budding grapes on the summer vines to the question of what treatments the wine should or shouldn't receive before bottling, that can make or break the reputations of producers. But has it become over-technologized? Is there just too much science involved in what should be a simple product?

The most extraordinary revolution in winemaking of recent times is the biodynamic movement. Not to be confused with straightforward organic production, which does away with chemical herbicide and pesticide sprays, biodynamic vineyard management is a quasi-mystical observance that involves consulting astrological star-charts, and such practices as the burying of a cow's horn full of dung in the middle of the vineyard over the winter to encourage the earth to regenerate for the coming growing season.

Now, I'm not one of those who believes in astrology, and there is an awful lot of undiluted gibberish uttered by biodynamic practitioners, which they can barely begin to justify rationally when pressed. On the other hand, taste the results in the glass, whether from Nicolas Joly in Savennières on the Loire, or from Millton Vineyards in New Zealand's Gisborne region, to name just two, and only a sceptic without tastebuds would deny that these are fabulous wines. Biodynamism will sweep the world in the coming generation, and if the wines continue to benefit as they have so far, we can only give thanks, however sceptically.

What else is new? Screwtops, once reserved only for the cheapest slosh, are now widespread. One can only regret that they didn't quite arrive in time to protect us all from synthetic corks, but now that they are here, they have eliminated the risk of taint from real cork. The incidence of corked wine was always blithely exaggerated by those who were against cork, but it is undeniable that a corked wine puts a major crimp in an evening. That said, there still isn't any better closure for a bottle that you're intending to age for several years, so reports of the death of cork have proved to be premature. They're replanting cork oak in the regions of Portugal where it was traditionally grown, and I for one wish them well in finding customers. It is, after all, a renewable resource.

A growing lament about the international standardization of wine styles addresses the most urgent issue of all. Too much wine tastes the same, overripe, full of fruit perhaps, but disappointingly one-dimensional, and with far, far too much alcohol – the last a result of the warming of the climate in many of the traditional wine regions. It can sometimes seem as though there are basically only three types of wine available now. At opposite ends of the spectrum are the sweet-tasting plonk of the big brands and the hyper-expensive prestige wines from global superstars old and new, with a huge, undifferentiated swathe of perfectly drinkable but soulless identikit stuff for the rest of us in the middle.

That's too pessimistic a picture, perhaps, but to look at what's on offer these days in the high-street retailers of the UK and North America doesn't do a great deal to convince you otherwise. The ranges are narrow, the flavours on offer monotonously similar, and the trade is geared to special offers of branded wines that virtually sell themselves anyway. More than ever, it makes sense to shop at the independent wine merchants. Browse their lists online (with this book to hand, of course), and let the experts tell you something you *don't* know once in a while.

Before too long, there will be more wine-producing countries in the world than can be fitted into a book of this size. I await developments in China with particular interest, having recently tasted some thoroughly exciting Xinjiang Province reds in Beijing. There are great wines being made in all styles, albeit on a small scale, on Malta, and Georgia and Ukraine are teeming with stirring, hearty reds. Exciting times lie ahead for the adventurous.

The first part of this book deals with keeping, serving and tasting wine. There is advice on professional tasting techniques and a guide to analysing the elements that make up a wine's aroma and flavour. Next comes information on where to store wine, what to open it with, whether or not to let it breathe and how to decant those wines that need it. A comparative look at different types of wine glass is followed by a general guide to matching wine and food. A final section gives pointers to the types of information presented on wine labels.

The second part takes a look at 12 of the most important grape varieties used in international winemaking. I have tried to give an indication of the different regional styles

each grape takes on, how the wines typically taste, and also an overview of the current debates surrounding each one, so that you can make up your own mind where you stand.

Armed with this knowledge, I hope you will continue to taste and try as broad a range of different wines as possible. That remains the best way that all of us can both celebrate and sustain the copious diversity that wine was always intended to be about. Happy drinking.

Stuart Walton

The vintage has traditionally been one of the ceremonial high points of the year in Europe's wine-growing regions, as this illustration from the medieval Book of Hours, c.1520 (above) vividly demonstrates.

PRINCIPLES *of* TASTING

All that sniffing, swirling and spitting that the professional winetasters engage in is more than just a way of showing off; it really can immeasurably enhance the appreciation of any wine.

WATCHING A PROFESSIONAL winetaster at work, you could be forgiven for wondering whether they really like wine at all. The ritual of peering into the glass, swirling it around and then sniffing suspiciously at it, before taking a mouthful only to spit it out again, doesn't look much like the behaviour of someone who loves the stuff. It is, however, a sequence of perfectly logical steps that, quite apart from helping you evaluate a wine's quality, can also immeasurably enhance the enjoyment of good wine. Here's how.

When pouring a tasting sample, be sure to leave enough room in the glass for giving it a good swirl (below).

Don't pour a full glass for tasting, because you're going to need room for swirling. About a third full is the optimum amount.

Firstly, have a good look at the wine by holding it up to the daylight or other light source. Is it nice and clear? Does it contain sediment or any other solid matter? In the case of red wines, tilt the glass away from you against a white surface, and look at the colour of the liquid at the far edge. Older wines start to fade at the rim, the deep purplish-red taking on lighter crimson tones, and later an autumnal brownish hue with dignified old age.

Now swirl the glass gently. The point of this is to activate the aromatic compounds in the wine, so that when you stick your nose in, you can fully appreciate the bouquet. The aim is to get a fairly vigorous wave circulating in the glass. Some people swirl the glass while it's still resting on a surface, before bringing it to their nose, but make sure the surface isn't likely to damage any good glassware.

When sniffing, tilt the glass towards your face and get your nose slightly inside it, keeping it within the lower half of the opening of the glass. The head should be bent forward a little. Inhale gently (as if you were sniffing a flower, not filling your lungs on a blustery clifftop) and for a good two or three seconds. Nosing a wine can reveal a lot about its origins and the way it was made, but don't overdo it. The sense of smell is quickly neutralized. Two or three sniffs should tell you as much as you need to know.

Now for the tricky part. The reason that wine experts pull those ridiculous faces when they take a mouthful is that they are trying to spread the wine all around the different taste-sensitive parts of the tongue. At its very tip, the receptors for sweetness are most densely concentrated. Just a little back from those, saltiness is registered. Acidity or sourness is tasted on the edges of the tongue, while bitterness is sensed at the very back. So roll the wine around your mouth as thoroughly as you can.

It helps to maximize the flavour of a wine if you take in air while it's in your mouth. Using gentle suction with the lips pursed, draw in some breath. Allow only the tiniest opening (less than the width of a pencil), and suck in immediately. Close your lips again, and breathe downwards through your nose. In this way, the flavour of the wine is transmitted past the taste receptors in your nasal cavity, as well as via your tongue, intensifying the whole sensation.

In polite company, swallow it. If you are tasting a number of wines at a time of day when you wouldn't normally be drinking, say at a market or fair, spit it out into whatever receptacle is provided (the ground will do). Spit confidently, with the tongue behind the ejected liquid, and spit downwards.

There are five principal elements to look for in the taste of a wine. Learn to concentrate on each one individually, and you will start to assemble a set of analytical tools that will stand you in good stead for evaluating any wine.

Dryness/Sweetness From a bone-dry Sancerre at one end of the spectrum to the most unctuous Liqueur Muscats at the other, the amount of natural sugar a wine contains is its most easily noted attribute.

Acidity There are many different types of acid in wine, the most important of which is tartaric, which is present in unfermented grape juice. How sharp does it feel on the edges of the tongue? Good acidity is necessary to contribute a feeling of freshness to a young wine, and to help the best wines to age. Don't confuse dryness with acidity. A very dry wine like fino sherry can actually be quite low in acid, while the sweetest Sauternes will contain sufficient acidity to offset its sugar.

Tannin Tannin is present in the stalks, seeds and skins of grapes. Since the colour in red wine comes from the skins (the juice being colourless), some tannin is extracted along with it. In the mouth, it's what gives young red wines that furry, sandy or abrasive feel, but it disappears with age.

Oak Many wines are matured (and sometimes even fermented too) in oak barrels. An aroma or taste of vanilla, nutmeg or cinnamon is an indicator of oak in white wines, and an overall feeling of creamy smoothness in richer reds. A pronounced smokiness like slightly burned toast indicates that the barrels were heavily charred (or 'toasted') on the insides.

Fruit We're all familiar with wine writers' flights of fancy ('I'm getting raspberries, passion-fruit, melon…'), but there are sound biochemical reasons for the resemblance of

wines to the flavours of fruits, vegetables, herbs and spices. We'll come across these in the Grape Varieties section, but let your imagination off the leash when tasting. Bright fruit flavours are among the great charms of wine.

Faults Not everything in the garden is lovely, and sometimes wines can display problems. Cork taint, leading to corked wine, bestows a nasty, stale aroma of old dishcloth or bread mould, but is much less widespread now that screwcaps have begun to replace real cork. Older wines can sometimes show oxidation, which deepens the colour of white wines alarmingly, and makes all wines taste flat and dead. Take back any wine that shows either of these faults. Sometimes tartrate crystals can be present in an imperfectly stabilized wine, but these don't affect its drinking quality.

A gentle swirling action of the hand is sufficient to produce quite a vigorous wave in the glass (above).

Wait for the mousse to subside in a sparkling wine before tasting it (above).
The different shades of colour in wine can convey a lot of information to the taster (below).

Sniff lightly and long, with the nose slightly below the rim of the glass (above).

Take a good mouthful of the wine, in order to coat all surfaces of the mouth with it (above).

STORING *and* SERVING

Where is the best place to keep wine for maturation? Should it be allowed to breathe before being served? What does decanting an old wine involve? None of these questions is as technical as it seems.

NONE OF THE TECHNICALITIES involved in the storage and serving of wine needs to be too complicated. The following guidelines are aimed at keeping things simple.
Creating a cellar Starting a wine collection requires a certain amount of ingenuity now that most of us live in flats or houses without cellars. If you have bought a large parcel of wine that you don't want to touch for years, you can pay a nominal fee to a wine merchant to cellar it for you, but the chances are that you may only have a couple of dozen bottles at any one time. Where to keep it?

The two main points to bear in mind are that bottles should be stored horizontally and away from sources of heat. You can pile them on top of each other if they are all the same shape, but it's safer and more convenient to invest in a simple wooden or plastic wine rack. Keeping the bottles on their sides means the wine is in constant contact with the corks, preventing them from drying out and imparting off-flavours to the wine.

Don't put your bottles in the cupboard next to the storage heater or near the cooker because heat is a menace to wine. Equally, don't leave it in the garden shed in sub-zero temperatures.

A simple wine rack is much the best way of storing bottles (right). This one allows enough space to see the labels too, so that they don't have to be pulled out to identify them.

Choose a cool cupboard that's not too high up (remember that heat rises) and where it can rest in peace in the dark.

Serving temperatures The conventional wisdom that white wine should be served chilled and red wine at room temperature is essentially correct, but it isn't the whole story.

Don't over-chill white wine or its flavours will be muted. Light, acidic whites, sparkling wines and very sweet wines (and rosés too for that matter) should be served at no higher than about 10°C (50°F) but the best Chardonnays, dry Semillons and Alsace wines can afford to be a little less cool than that.

Reds, on the other hand, generally benefit from being slightly cooler than the ambient temperature in a well-heated home. Never warm the bottle by a radiator as that will make the wine taste muddy. Some lighter, fruity reds such as young Beaujolais, Dolcetto or the lighter

Loire or New Zealand reds are best served lightly chilled – about an hour in the refrigerator.

Breathing Should red wine be allowed to breathe? In the case of matured reds that are intended to be drunk on release, like Rioja Reservas or the softer, barrel-aged Cabernet Sauvignons of Australia, the answer is that there is probably no point. Young reds with some tannin, or immature hard acidity, do round out with a bit of air contact, though. Either pour the wine into a decanter or jug (pitcher) half an hour or so before serving or, if you haven't anything suitable for the table, pour it into another container and then funnel it back into the bottle. Simply drawing the cork won't in itself make any difference because only the wine in the neck is in contact with the air. And remember the wine will develop in any case in the glass as you keep swirling and slowly sipping it.

Here is an ingeniously designed wine rack that ensures that the undersides of the corks are kept constantly in contact with the wine, thus preventing them from drying out.

Corkscrews With the increasing use of the Stelvin closure (aka the screwcap) for all quality levels of wine – pioneered in the southern hemisphere, but now widely in use in Europe too – you can leave the corkscrew in the drawer. The great advantage is that any leftover wine can be easily resealed, and of course there is no risk of cork taint.

For corks, the spin-handled corkscrew is the easiest to use, because it involves one continuous motion, and very little effort. The type with side-levers is less good, because it often needs two or three attempts with longer corks, and can break a fragile cork in two, especially if it's the type with a solid shaft as opposed to a hollow spiral. The simplest model, the Wine Waiter's Friend, is good for those who like displaying their brute strength, but an obstinate cork can reduce you to a study in red-faced futility.

The Spin-handled Screwpull (above) was the corkscrew that revolutionized the business of bottle opening. Not only does it require very little in the way of brute force, but it virtually never breaks a cork in two. That is because the screw itself (or thread) is so long.

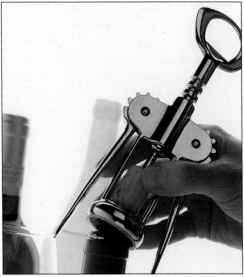

The most basic type of corkscrew (above left) involves simply tugging. The levered model (above right) can sometimes break a long or old cork. A bottle with a screwcap (right) avoids the need for any sort of special implement at all. There are now three kinds of bottle closure (far right): natural cork, synthetic cork and the Stelvin or screwcap.

Avoid if you can any wines sealed with synthetic cork. When they get stuck, they stay stuck. They are the only closure that won't go back in the bottle, and they can break a plastic corkscrew. Briefly seen as the alternative to real cork some years ago, they have now thankfully begun to be widely superseded as a technology by more efficient screwcaps.

Opening fizz Many people are still intimidated about opening sparkling wines. Remember that the longer a bottle of fizz has been able to rest before opening, the less lively it will be. If it has been very badly shaken up, it may need a week or more to settle. Also, the colder it is, the less likely it will be to go off like a firecracker.

Once the foil has been removed and the wire cage untwisted and taken off too, grasp the cork firmly and take hold of the lower half of the bottle. The advice generally given is to turn the bottle rather than the cork, but in practice most people probably do both (twisting in opposite directions, of course). Work very gently and, when you feel or see the cork beginning to rise, control it every millimetre of the way with your thumb over the top. It should be possible then to ease it out without it popping. If the wine does spurt, put a finger in the neck, but don't completely stopper it again.

When pouring, fill each glass to just under half-full, and then go round again to top them up once the initial fizz has subsided. Pour fairly slowly so that the wine doesn't foam over the sides. Pouring into tilted glasses does preserve more of the fizz, though some see it as vulgarly reminiscent of pouring lager.

Decanting Decanting can help to make a tough young wine a bit more supple, but it is only absolutely necessary if the wine being served is heavily sedimented. In that case, stand the bottle upright for the best part of the day you intend to serve it (from the night before is even better) so that the deposits settle to the bottom. After uncorking, pour the wine in a slow but continuous stream into the decanter, looking into the neck of the bottle. When the sediment starts working its way into the neck as you reach the end, stop pouring. The amount of wine you are left with should be negligible enough to throw away, but if there's more than half a glass, then strain the remainder through a clean muslin cloth. Do *not* use coffee filter-papers or tissue as they will alter the flavour of the wine. Decanting is particularly essential for old bottles of vintage port.

When opening sparkling wines, it is important to restrain the release of the cork (left). Control it every millimetre of the way once it begins to push out.

The quicker you pour, the more vigorous will be the foaming of the wine in the glass (left). Pour carefully to avoid any wastage through overflowing.

The Champagne Saver is a good way of preserving the fizz in any unfinished bottles of sparkling wine (left). Some swear, quite unscientifically, by inserting a spoon-handle in the neck.

GLASSES

Wine doesn't have to be served in the most expensive glassware to show it to advantage, but there are a few basic principles to bear in mind when choosing glasses that will help you get the best from your bottle.

Glasses these days come in all shapes and sizes (below). From left to right in the foreground are: a good red or white wine glass; a technically correct champagne flute; the famous 'Paris goblet' much beloved of wine-bars, not a bad shape but too small; an elegant-looking but inefficient sparkling wine glass with flared opening, causing greater dispersal of bubbles; a sherry copita, *also useful for other fortified wines.*

ALTHOUGH I CAN scarcely remember any champagne that tasted better than the stuff we poured into polystyrene cups huddled in my student quarters after the examination results went up, the truth is that, certainly when you're in the mood to concentrate, it does make a difference what you drink wine from. Not only the appearance but the scent and even the taste of wine can be substantially enhanced by using appropriate glasses.

They don't have to be prohibitively costly, although – as with everything else – the best doesn't come cheap. The celebrated Austrian glassmaker Georg Riedel has taken the science of wine glasses to its ultimate degree, working out what design features will emphasize the specific aromatic and flavour compounds in dozens of different types of wine. Some of

them are very peculiar shapes and they're expensive, but they undeniably do the trick.

There are some broad guidelines we can all follow, however, when choosing glasses. Firstly, always choose a plain glass to set off your best wines. Coloured ones, or even those with just the stems and bases tinted, can distort the appearance of white wines particularly. And, although cut crystal can look very beautiful, it has now fallen from fashion. I tend to avoid it for wines because it doesn't make for the clearest view of the liquid in the glass.

Look for a deep, wide bowl that tapers significantly towards the mouth. With such glasses, the aromas of the wine can be released more generously, both because the deeper bowl allows for more vigorous swirling, and because the narrower opening channels the scents of the

wine to your nostrils more efficiently. Also, the thinner the glass it's made from, the less it will interfere with tasting.

Traditionally, red wine is served in bigger glasses than white. If you are serving both colours at a grand gastronomic evening, it helps to allot different wines their individual glasses, but the assumption is that reds, especially mature wines, need more space in which to breathe. More development of the wine will take place in the glass than in any decanter or jug you may have poured it into. If you are only buying one size, though, think big. A wine glass can never be too large.

Sparkling wines should be served in flutes, tall thin glasses with straight sides, so that the mousse or fizz is preserved. The champagne saucers familiar from old movies (and originally modelled, as legend has it, on the breast of Marie Antoinette) are less efficient because the larger surface area of the wine causes faster dispersal of the bubbles. That said, they have defiantly come back into fashion in some quarters, and I have to own up to a guilty fondness for their elegance myself.

Fortified wines should be served in smaller, narrower versions of the ordinary wine glass, in recognition of their higher alcoholic strength. The *copita*, traditional glass of the sherry region, is a particularly handsome receptacle, and will do quite well for the other fortifieds too. Don't use your tiniest liqueur glasses: apart from looking spectacularly mean, they allow no room for enjoying the wine's aromas.

These three glasses (left) are all perfectly shaped for tasting. The one on the right is the official international tasting-glass.

DRINKING WINE *with* FOOD

Matching the right wine to its appropriate dish may seem like a gastronomic assault course but there are broad principles that can be easily learned. And very few mistakes are complete failures.

AT ONE TIME, the rules on choosing wines to accompany food seemed hearteningly simple. It was just a matter of remembering: white wine with fish and poultry, red wine with red meats and cheese, with sherry to start and port to finish. Recent thinking has hugely complicated that basic picture, although its essential principles remain sound.

What is clear is that this is one of those areas in which there are no fixed rules. Even though a particular dish may be a firm favourite, why drink the same wine with it every time? Whenever I go to tastings of wine with food, there are always at least a couple of matches that are completely surprising successes.

The following are rough guidelines that are intended to send you off in some new directions. On the whole, you can afford to be bold: very few combinations actually clash.

Pre-dinner nibbles with strong flavours such as prawns (shrimp), tomato, hollandaise sauce, watercress, avocado, salmon and coriander (cilantro) (below) are best served with either a chilled fino or manzanilla sherry or a fresh, young dry white wine, such as an unoaked Chardonnay.

APERITIFS

The two classic (and best) appetite-whetters are sparkling wine and dry sherry. Choose a light, non-vintage champagne (blanc de blancs has the requisite delicacy), or one of the lighter California or New Zealand sparklers. If you are serving highly seasoned canapés, olives or nuts before the meal, dry sherry is better. Always serve a freshly opened bottle of good fino or manzanilla. Kir has become quite trendy again: add a dash of cassis (blackcurrant liqueur) to a glass of crisp dry white – classically Bourgogne Aligoté – or to bone-dry fizz for a Kir Royale.

FIRST COURSES

Soups In general, liquidized soups are happier without wine, although thickly textured versions containing cream or truffle oil work with richer styles of fizz, such as blanc de noirs

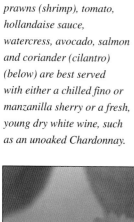

Chicken and pistachio pâté with crusty bread (above) is best with a white wine that has some aromatic personality, perhaps a Torrontes.

champagne. A small glass of one of the nuttier-tasting fortified wines such as amontillado sherry or Sercial madeira is a good friend to a meaty consommé. Bulky chowders and minestrones may benefit from a medium-textured red – perhaps a Montepulciano d'Abruzzo – to kick off a winter dinner.

Fish pâtés Light dry whites without overt fruit are best: Chablis, Alsace Pinot Blanc, Muscadet *sur lie*, Spanish Viura, South African Chenin Blanc, shading to something a little richer, such as Spain's Rias Baixas, with the oilier fish like smoked mackerel.

Chicken, duck or pork liver pâtés Go for a big, pungently flavoured white – Alsace Gewurztraminer, dry Bordeaux from Pessac-Léognan, Hunter Valley Semillon. The traditional partner for foie gras is Sauternes (which I find much too sickly a combination).

Smoked salmon Needs a hefty white such as Gewurztraminer or Pinot Gris from Alsace, or an oak-fermented Chardonnay from the Côte de Beaune or California. Beware: champagne will wither under the onslaught of salt, smoke and fat, however traditional it seems.

Melon The sweeter-fleshed aromatic varieties require a wine with its own gentle sweetness. Try late-picked Muscat or Riesling from Washington or California, or even young Canadian Ice Wine.

Prawns, shrimp, langoustines, etc Almost any crisp dry white will work – Sauvignon Blanc is a good grape to choose – but avoid heavily oaked wines. Go for high acidity if you are serving mayonnaise or garlic butter.

Deep-fried mushrooms Best with a midweight simple red such as Côtes du Rhône, Valdepeñas or Valpolicella.

Asparagus Richer styles of Sauvignon, such as those from New Zealand, are perfect.

Pasta dishes and risottos These really are best with Italian wines. Choose a concentrated white such as Vernaccia, Arneis, Falanghina or good Soave for cream sauces, or dishes involving seafood. Light- to medium-bodied reds from Italian grapes (Barbera, Montepulciano) work best with tomato-based sauces. A wild mushroom risotto with Parmesan is great with one of the richer styles of Chianti.

FISH AND SHELLFISH

Oysters Classic partners are champagne, Muscadet or Chablis. Most unoaked Sauvignon also makes a suitably bracing match.

Scallops Simply poached or seared, this most delicate of shellfish needs a soft light white – Côte Chalonnaise burgundy, medium-dry German or New Zealand Riesling, Italian Pinot Grigio – becoming correspondingly richer, the creamier the sauce.

Salt-cured salmon (above) needs a white wine with plenty of weight, such as an Alsace Gewurztraminer or a Pinot Gris.

Salmon Goes well with elegant, midweight whites with some acidity, such as *premier cru* Chablis, Chilean Chardonnay, dry Rieslings from Alsace or Germany. Equally, it is capable of taking a lightish red such as Côte de Beaune Pinot Noir.

Tuna Go for a fairly assertive red in preference to white: well-built Pinot Noir (California or New Zealand), mature Loire red (Chinon or Bourgueil), Chilean Merlot.

Sushi and sashimi What else but sake?

MEAT AND POULTRY

Chicken If roasted, go for a soft-edged quality red, such as mature burgundy, Rioja Crianza or California Merlot. Lighter treatments such as poaching may need one of the richer whites, depending on any sauce.

Turkey The Christmas or Thanksgiving turkey deserves a show-stopping red with a little more power than you would serve with roast chicken: St-Emilion claret, Châteauneuf-du-Pape, California Cabernet.

Rabbit As for roast chicken.

Pork Roast pork or grilled chops are happiest with fairly full reds with a touch of spice: southern Rhône blends, Australian Shiraz, Chianti Classico.

Lamb The two best mates are Cabernet Sauvignon (Médoc, Napa, Chile, etc) and Rioja Reserva.

Lobster Thermidor (above) is best with a rich, ideally oak-aged white. Best white burgundy or hot-climate Chardonnay are ideal.

Rabbit dishes (right) will take either red or white wines, depending on the treatment. A rich white would be good with mustard sauce, while Pinot Noir would work well alongside rabbit with red wine and prunes.

Lobster Cold in a salad, it needs a pungent white with some acidity, such as Pouilly-Fumé, dry Vouvray, Chablis *premier cru*, South African Chenin Blanc, Australian Riesling. Served hot as a main course (e.g. Thermidor), it requires an opulent and heavier wine – Meursault, California or South Australian Chardonnay, Alsace Pinot Gris.

Light-textured white fish Sole, lemon sole, plaice and the like go well with any light, unoaked or very lightly oaked white from almost anywhere.

Firm-fleshed fish Fish like sea bass, brill, turbot, tilapia or cod need full-bodied whites to match their texture. *Cru classé* white Bordeaux, Australian Semillon, and most of the richer Chardonnays of the southern hemisphere will fit the bill.

Monkfish Either a weighty white such as Hermitage or top burgundy, or – if cooked in red wine or wrapped in ham – something quite beefy such as Moulin-à-Vent or Rioja Crianza.

Beef Rump or sirloin can cope with the burliest reds from anywhere: Hermitage, the sturdiest Zinfandels, Barolo, Coonawarra Shiraz. A little lighter for fillet: South African Merlot, Bordeaux. Peppered steaks, mustard sauces and horseradish all demand a wine with bite, perhaps Crozes-Hermitage.

Duck A midweight red with youthful acidity to cut the fat is best: Chianti Classico, Zinfandel, New Zealand Pinot.

Game birds Best with fully mature Pinot Noir.

Venison Highly concentrated reds with some bottle-age are good. Cabernet, Shiraz or Zinfandel from hotter climates work well.

Offal Liver and kidneys are good with vigorous young reds such as Chinon, Barbera or *cru* Beaujolais. Sweetbreads are better with a high-powered white such as a mature Alsace.

Indian Fruity whites with a cutting-edge of acidity (Chenin, Riesling) are best with highly spiced dishes, but go red (Cabernet, Merlot) for lamb dishes like rogan josh.

Thai The chilli heat and abundance of lime and ginger make Sauvignon Blanc the surefire choice, whether from Sancerre, South Africa or New Zealand.

Chinese Perfumed whites such as Gewurztraminer, Viognier, Argentinian Torrontés and most Riesling are good cover-all wines for the huge diversity of Chinese food.

DESSERTS

Fresh fruit salads are best served on their own, on account of their natural acidity. Similarly, frozen desserts like ice-creams and sorbets tend to numb the palate's sensitivity to wine. Anything based on eggs and cream, such as mousses, crème brûlée and pannacotta, deserves a noble-rotted wine such as Sauternes, Coteaux du Layon, or equivalent wines from outside Europe. Chocolate, often thought to present problems, doesn't do much damage to botrytized wines, but think maximum richness and high alcohol. Fruit tarts are better with a late-picked rather than fully rotted wine, such as Auslese German or Austrian Riesling, Alsace Vendange Tardive, or late-harvest South African Muscat. Meringues and creamy gâteaux are good with the sweeter styles of sparkling wine, while Asti or Moscato d'Asti make refreshing counter-balances to Christmas pudding. Sweet oloroso sherry, Bual or Malmsey madeira and Australian Liqueur Muscat are all superb with rich, dark fruitcake or anything nutty such as pecan pie.

The classic partner for boeuf bourguinonne (left) is a soft, mature burgundy – the region from which the dish originated.

Mince pies with orange whisky butter (below) could be paired either with sparkling Italian Asti, or with a marmaladey Australian Liqueur Muscat.

LABELLING

Champagne labels are rarely complicated. The house name will always dominate, since it is a form of brand, in this case Billecart-Salmon at Mareuil-sur-Ay. Below is the style, Brut being virtually the driest, and this one is pink. Champagne is the only AC wine that doesn't require the words *appellation contrôlée* to appear. Along the bottom, the reference number of this house denotes that it is an NM (*négociant-manipulant*), a producer that buys in grapes and makes its own wine.

The most prominent detail on a Bordeaux label is the property at which the wine was made. A classed growth always announces itself with the formula "*cru classé* en 1855". Lower down, the sub-region from which the wine hails is stated, in this case St-Julien, which also forms the name of the appellation.

Burgundy labelling can be a minefield. The merchant's name (Drouhin) is followed by the appellation. This label tells you this is a *grand cru* wine, but doesn't have to state which village it belongs to (Morey-St-Denis, in fact). Note that *mis en bouteille* is not followed by *au domaine*, because it has not been bottled on an individual estate, but by a négociant based elsewhere.

Reading down this Italian label, we have the name of the vineyard (Vigna del Sorbo), then the producer (Fontodi) and then the appellation or denominazione (Chianti Classico). Then comes the quality level – Italy's highest, DOCG. Riserva denotes a wine aged for at least three years before release. Below is the information that the wine was bottled at the estate by its producer.

The practised eye begins to discern similarities among the labels of different European countries. On this Spanish label, we see the name of the producer (La Rioja Alta SA), then the appellation or denominación (Rioja), and the standard formula that announces its quality level – DOCa, Spain's highest. Under the vintage comes the wine name. Gran Reserva denotes a wine that has been kept for five years before release, of which at least two must be spent in oak, 904 being a kind of brand name for this producer's top wines. *Embotellado en la propiedad* means 'bottled on the estate'.

German labels can look even more fiendishly complicated than the French. Underneath the proprietor's name here (Dr Pauly-Bergweiler), we have what amounts to the designated appellation. This one comes specifically from the Alte Badstube am Doctorberg vineyard in the village of Bernkastel on the Mosel, which happens to be solely owned by this producer, and is so called because it adjoins the famous Bernkasteler Doctor vineyard. This is roughly comparable within the classification structure – and also in size – to a tiny *grand cru* within one of the village appellations of Burgundy (say, the Romanée-Conti vineyard of Vosne-Romanée). Next to the vintage date, we are told the grape variety is Riesling, and the style of this wine is Spätlese (late-picked). In the absence of any other qualifier, we can therefore take it to be very delicately sweet in style. A dry version would be labelled Spätlese Trocken.

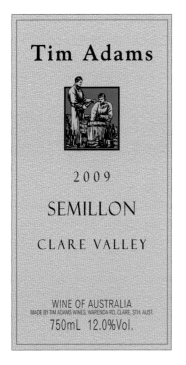

In the sometimes complex world of bottle labelling, what could be simpler than the information on this varietal wine from an acclaimed South Australia producer? The proprietor has given his own name to the estate, which appears prominently at the top (Tim Adams), with the vintage (2009), grape variety (Semillon) and region (Clare Valley) following on below it. In essence, this is pretty much what that German label is also telling you, but notice how much more straightforward the Australian label looks.

This label simply tells us the name of the estate (Thelema), the vintage year (2007), the grape variety (Merlot) and the region of the country in which it was grown and produced (Stellenbosch). Even though there is a regional denomination system in South Africa, the label itself still manages to be crystal-clear.

GRAPE VARIETIES

Soil is furrowed the ancient way to catch winter rain (above), in the sweltering south of Spain.

Such is the mystique and reverence attached to the appreciation of wine that it is easy to forget just what a simple product it is.

Visiting a modern winery today, with its acres of carefully trained vines, the giant tanks of shining stainless steel, the automated bottling line, and perhaps the rows of oak barrels resting on top of one another in deep cavernous cellars, you might think this was the end product of centuries of human ingenuity.

To the extent that the techniques for making good wine have been steadily refined through succeeding generations, indeed it is. Unlike beer, though, which had to await the discovery of malting grains before it could be produced, the rudiments of wine have always been there, for it is nothing other than spoiled grape juice.

Any substance that is high in natural sugars – whether it be the sticky sap of palm trees, or honey, or the juice of ripened fruit – will sooner or later start to ferment if it comes into contact with yeast. Wild yeasts, transported on the bodies of insects and falling on to the fruit that they hover around, feed on the fruit sugar and initiate fermentation, creating two principal by-products in the process.

One is carbon dioxide gas, which is why anything that has accidentally started fermenting tastes slightly fizzy, and the other is alcohol. And we know what that does to us.

Long before the earliest human societies had begun to live settled rather than nomadic existences, and begun to cultivate the land, a basic type of alcoholic drink could be derived from the controlled fermentation of fresh fruit or honey. This was the prototype of wine.

One particular species of wild vine, which originated in the area around the Black Sea that today takes in Georgia, Armenia and eastern Turkey, proved especially well suited to quick fermentation, owing to the naturally sweet berries it produced. It is in fact the only vine species native to Europe and the Near East and, because it came to play such a pre-eminent role in the development of winemaking all over the world, it was later given the botanical classification *Vitis vinifera* – 'the wine-bearing grape'.

Within that one species, however, there are as many as 10,000 different sub-types, known as varieties. Some of these developed by natural mutation; many have been created by deliberate cross-fertilization. Only a small percentage of those 10,000 are important in the commercial production of wine today (the French wine authorities recognize around 200), and many of those are fairly obscure and consequently hardly ever used. A mere handful, overwhelmingly French in origin, now constitutes the international language of wine, and it is these that this section deals with.

A breathtaking springtime scene (right),with flowering mustard seed growing in the vineyards of Sonoma, California, the state that has become a major player on the world wine scene.

Not all of the 12 varieties we'll look at are grown throughout the world, and the last of them – Gamay – is mostly concentrated in its own little corner of France (Beaujolais). But these are the 12 varieties – seven white and five red – whose flavours it is most useful to become familiar with. They are responsible between them for producing all the most famous French wine styles, from champagne in the north to the richly heady reds of the sweltering south, and they therefore provided the original models when serious winemaking first began to be pioneered beyond the shores of Europe.

All the European countries have indigenous grapes of their own, some of which have made it on to the international wine scene. There are plantings of some of the best Spanish, Italian and Portuguese grapes in North and South America, and in the enterprising wine cultures of Australia and New Zealand. We begin in this section, though, with the French grapes (plus Germany's Riesling), because those have been the earliest and most widely travelled ones.

All sorts of factors influence the taste of wine. The climate in which the grapes are grown; the type of soil in the vineyards; the way the vines are trained and managed during the growing season; the temperature at which the juice is fermented; what it ferments in (stainless steel or wood); how much contact red

wines have with the grape-skins; the duration and type of any cask-ageing. But nothing affects the style more importantly than the grape or grapes the wine is made from.

There are as many styles of wine as there are winemakers, an equation augmented by the number of different vintages each practitioner will oversee during his or her career. But the identity of the grapes in the fermenting vat is the first and foremost determinant of taste.

If you want to drink a delicately crisp, simple white, it doesn't make sense to go for Gewürztraminer. Similarly, if you're after a featherlight, fruity red for a summer's day, you may get more than you bargained for from Cabernet Sauvignon. The most widely met grape varieties have innate common characteristics.

As we are introduced to each of these 12 VIPs of the wine world, we shall also take a look at the different regions in which they feature, both at home and abroad, and explore the typical styles and flavours to be found in each of them.

The impressive vaulted cellars of Ch. de Meursault, in Burgundy's Côte de Beaune (above), filled with wine ageing in oak barrels.

CHARDONNAY

From its homeland in Burgundy, Chardonnay has travelled the world to become the most fashionable and sought-after of white varieties. This chameleon of grapes bows to the whim of the winemaker, offering a diversity of styles to appeal to all palates.

A S SOMEBODY once (nearly) said, if Chardonnay didn't exist, it would be necessary to invent it. No other grape, white or red, has even now achieved quite the degree of international recognition that Chardonnay has. In many consumers' minds, it stands as a synonym for dry white wine in general, and the reason is not hard to find. It is grown is some proportion in virtually every wine-producing country on the planet.

Its adaptablity in the vineyard and its almost limitless mutability in the winery are what made Chardonnay the first big success story among grape varieties. Compared with most other major grapes, it is relatively easy to grow. It can take a wide spectrum of climatic conditions in its stride, from the pinched summers of northern France to the broiling sun-traps of South Australia, and it isn't especially fussy about the kinds of soils it grows in. It ripens well, and it yields plentifully in most vintages. While it's true that great wines are for the most part produced from low-yielding vines, the truth is that the vast bulk of worldwide Chardonnay is destined for straightforward, everyday wines that are intended to be drunk young.

Just as Chardonnay has been everybody's flexible friend in the vineyard, so it proves similarly malleable in the winery. It isn't in itself an especially characterful variety (although there are certain sub-types of it that do have some intriguingly musky perfume), hence its suitability for everyday drinking. On the other hand, it is precisely that innate neutrality that fits it so well – perhaps more obviously than any other white variety – for responding to oak treatments.

Given even a short period of maturation in oak barrels, whether new or used once or twice already, it begins to take on some of those buttery or vanilla scents we classically associate with premium Chardonnay. Ferment it in barrel to begin with, with a further period of ageing in the cask, and those buttery notes are backed up by savoury, toasty aromas. If the insides of the barrels have been given a thorough charring, we may end up with something that is, in effect, smoked wine.

Various economic shortcuts to impart the taste of oak to a wine can be used by producers keen to avoid the outlay of putting their Chardonnays through an expensive finishing-school. A 'chipped' Chardonnay has had a bag of oak chippings (something like a giant teabag) macerated in the wine. One that has been 'staved' has been held in specially designed steel vats that incorporate vertical strips of oak on their inner surfaces. All of which is far cheaper than investing in a consignment of new barrels every year.

Chardonnay matures in the warm vineyards of California (right). A vigorous vine, relatively unfussed by climate or soil, this golden grape is neutral in character and has a natural affinity with oak. It is as suited to classic white burgundies as to Australian sparkling wines.

With the asset of huge popularity comes the liability of changing fashion. In the years since the 1990s, Chardonnay has undergone something of a rocky period in consumers' affections. The international palate eventually grew fatigued with wines that tasted as though the oak had been laid on with a trowel. Australia's Chardonnays (a little unfairly) were suddenly seen as the prime culprits, leading to the wholesale abandonment there of oak-ageing at the simpler end of the spectrum. Suddenly, labels proudly proclaimed their Chardonnays to be 'unoaked', as though they were being declared free of some adulterating substance.

While that welcome development certainly led to a generation of more finely balanced wines, it also contained within it a paradoxical drawback. As we learned above, Chardonnay is an extremely simple wine when it doesn't have anything beyond basic vinification done to it. And the sudden worldwide preponderance of what were essentially rather prosaic, lightly lemony dry whites of no great personality is

what led to Chardonnay fatigue, best expressed by the emergence of a movement among dissenting drinkers in the United States known as ABC – Anything But Chardonnay.

The search was on for a white grape that could replicate some of the reliability of Chardonnay, while providing drinkers with something a little more idiosyncratic, a little more varied from one wine to the next, than Chardonnay is capable of. Viognier (see page 84) was where a lot of the smart money went, although the answer has turned out for the time being to lie more readily to hand in the shape of another already established variety, Sauvignon Blanc (see page 50).

As well as making one of the most famous styles of white table wine, Chardonnay is also indispensable to the production of quality sparkling wines the world over. It forms one of the triumvirate of grapes used in champagne, and nearly all producers of classic sparklers elsewhere have plantings of Chardonnay. Once again, it is the grape's inherent neutrality that bestows elegance and finesse on the best fizz.

FRENCH ORIGINS

Almost all of the white wines of Burgundy, from Chablis down to Beaujolais. Champagne (where it makes up 100 per cent of wines labelled blanc de blancs). May appear as varietally labelled *vin de pays* across the south, especially Languedoc, and also in the Loire.

WHERE ELSE IS IT GROWN?

Wherever the vine will grow.

TASTING NOTES

Light and unoaked (e.g. Chablis) – tart apple, lemon, sometimes pear. Lightly oaked (e.g. Rully, St-Véran) – melting butter, baked apple, nutmeg, oatmeal. Heavily oaked (e.g. Meursault, classic Australian Chardonnay) – vanilla, lemon curd, butterscotch, praline, bacon fat, woodsmoke.

Burgundy

If Chardonnay represents the monarch among white wine grapes, then the Burgundy region in eastern France is its official residence. From the isolated enclave of Chablis in the *département* of the Yonne down to the wide swathes of vineyard known as the Mâconnais to the west of the river Saône, Chardonnay is the overwhelmingly predominant white grape variety.

The entire gamut of styles is produced. There are easy-drinking, everyday whites of honest simplicity, as well as powerfully complex wines intended to be aged in the bottle. There are wines that rely on youthful acidity and freshness alone for their appeal, while others mobilize the fat buttery opulence imparted by oak.

Cooperatives and négociants (merchants who buy in grapes from growers under contract and bottle the resulting blend under their own name) tend to be the sources for much of the commercial white burgundy seen in high-street drinks outlets, while the many individual producers who operate entirely self-sufficiently are responsible for some of the world's most extravagantly rich – and extravagantly expensive – dry white wine.

Chablis in some ways deserves to be considered as a region in itself, because it is not geographically part of Burgundy proper, lying as it does slightly nearer to the most southerly part of the Champagne vineyards than to the northernmost tip of the Côte d'Or. Its climate is cool and fairly wet, its winters often severe, and late frosts in spring are a regular occurrence. Those conditions mean Chardonnay ripens quite late, tending to produce a high-acid wine, often described as steely.

At their best, these are squeaky-clean, bone-dry wines that can be crisp to the point of brittleness in their youth. As they age, they lose some of that sharp edge and become mellower. That said, there is a general tendency to make softer wine these days, which runs the risk that they lack bite when young, and don't mature with quite the same complexity as the traditional style.

The great majority of the wines are made without oak, Chablis being the original reference for the world's unwooded Chardonnays. Some producers, however, do use a certain amount of oak on their best *cuvées*, particularly those with land in one or more of the seven *grand cru* vineyards that sit at the top of the quality tree. Even without oak, Chablis from a good producer in a fine vintage (such as 2007 or 2009) can develop its own inherent richness, often tantalizingly hinting at some phantom oak presence, with a few years in the bottle.

Southeast of Chablis, white wines from the Côte d'Or – and in particular the Côte de Beaune, its southern stretch – represent the pinnacle of Burgundian Chardonnay. It is here, in the exalted appellations of Corton-Charlemagne, Puligny-Montrachet, Meursault and others, that oaked Chardonnay really began.

The top wines, often produced in tiny quantities selling at dizzyingly elevated prices, are sumptuously rich and concentrated, often deep golden in colour from months of ageing in oak barrels, and generally high in alcohol (13–13.5 per cent is the norm). Many possess an intriguingly vegetal flavour, like green beans, leeks or even cabbage, that can be something of a shock to

The rich, golden colours of a Burgundian autumn (below) spread through the sloping grand cru *vineyards of Vaudésir (nearest) and Grenouilles, in Chablis.*

those used to fruitier-tasting Chardonnays. The Burgundians argue that this is their famous *goût de terroir* – the unique taste of the limestone soils in which the vines are grown.

It is still fair to say that many winemakers aiming to produce premium-quality oaked Chardonnay began by looking to the top wines of the Côte d'Or for their original inspiration, however much they may since have diverged from that earliest model.

The Côte d'Or is connected to the Mâconnais by a strip of land called the Côte Chalonnaise, so called because it lies just to the west of the town of Chalon-sur-Saône. Its Chardonnays, from appellations such as Montagny, Rully and Mercurey, are considerably lighter in style than those from further north, but can possess their own lean elegance. They tend to have correspondingly less oak (if any) than the Côte d'Or wines, but as so often, certain individual producers can provide the exception to the rule.

In the south of Burgundy, the Mâconnais is the largest of the sub-regions. Here is where most of the everyday quaffing wine is made, much of it of rather humdrum quality, often vinified without oak. The best appellation, Pouilly-Fuissé, can have something of the depth

and ageability of lesser Côte de Beaune wines, while St-Véran is often as good as anything from the Chalonnaise.

Certain villages within the overall appellation of Mâcon Blanc-Villages are considered to produce wines of sufficiently distinct quality for their names to be added to the label (hence Mâcon-Lugny, Mâcon-Verzé, and so forth).

In recent years, some quality producers have taken to selling wine under the simplest appellation of all, Bourgogne Chardonnay, the result sufficiently full and rich (and perhaps oaky) as to belie the apparently humble designation – and also to allow them to compete on the shelves with Chardonnays from elsewhere.

The rare white wine of Beaujolais, Burgundy's southernmost sector, is Chardonnay too, a chalky-dry, usually unoaked style a little like a less graceful Chablis.

Burgundy's sparkling wine, Crémant de Bourgogne, made by the same method as champagne, relies principally on Chardonnay. The grapes can theoretically come from anywhere in the region, and the bottle maturation varies between producers, so styles run the range from overly delicate to something approximating the complex, yeasty fullness of champagne itself.

Hand-picked Chardonnay grapes are loaded on to a trailer at Fuissé (above) in the Mâconnais, the largest sub-region of Burgundy.

United States

Wineries in New York State, especially those on Long Island (above), are increasingly producing elegant, complex Chardonnays.

Undoubtedly, the most dynamic Chardonnay developments outside Europe have taken place in the United States. Indeed, by the end of the 1980s, the state of California alone had more extensive plantings of the grape than the whole of France, where its growth has not exactly been stagnant. No group of winemakers beyond the ancestral heartland of Burgundy has taken greater pains with the variety than the Californians, and the transformations that the wines have undergone in the last two decades have been a fascinating barometer of changing Chardonnay trends.

In the 1970s and 80s, the fashion was for a massively overblown style of rich golden wine, with dollops of sweet new oak all over it, not dissimilar to what was then the southern hemisphere mode. When the backlash came, it sent the pendulum hurtling in the other direction, so that it suddenly seemed as if everybody was competing to produce West Coast Chablis, so lean and green and biting were many of the wines.

By the late 1980s, the picture was beginning to even out, and there is now a much greater diversity of styles, each representing a more relaxed expression of its microclimate and the intentions of the individual winemaker.

The very best Stateside Chardonnays – such as those from the cooler areas of California like Carneros and Sonoma Valley, from Oregon and New York State – can sometimes achieve an almost eerie similarity to certain top burgundies, partly because of the comparable levels of acidity, and partly because of the sensitive use of new French oak.

A lot of work has been done in researching types of oak, and the different levels of flame treatment the cooper can give the barrels, to find out what best suits American Chardonnay. Some producers, veterans of field trips to Burgundy, put their faith in the flavours of French oak, but others have looked again at native American woods and have disproved the theory that you can't make a subtle Chardonnay in US oak.

Another French habit that has taken root among many of the premium producers is avoidance of the filtration procedure, in which microscopic solid residues of the fermentation are cleaned out of the wine. While filtering a wine certainly results in a crystal-clear, stable

Madonna Vineyards in the cool Carneros region of northern California (right), a region that produces some of the state's finest Chardonnays, eerily similar in style to certain top burgundies.

product, many feel that it also strips it of some of its flavour complexity and richness of texture. The anti-filtration brigade has often proudly inscribed the word 'Unfiltered' on the labels.

It is no more possible to generalize about a typical California style of Chardonnay than it is to talk about a French style. The state contains a multitude of different microclimates, reflected in the various AVAs (American Viticultural Areas, the equivalent of appellations): Calistoga, at the northern end of Napa Valley, is one of the hotter areas, as are the inland districts of San Joaquin, while Santa Ynez, to the south, is relatively cool.

Most of California's coastal regions are affected each day by Pacific fog drifts, which can take until mid-morning to clear. Those, and cool night-time conditions, help to ensure that the ripening grapes don't become heat-stressed, so that acidity levels at harvest-time are not too low.

Good California Chardonnays have the same sort of weight in the mouth as wines like Puligny-Montrachet, with a carefully defined balance of oak and fruit. Acidity is usually fresh, though with perhaps not quite the same tang as young burgundy. Owing to the specific clonal types of the grape favoured, the fruit flavours are altogether more overt, California wines often having a riper citrus character

(mandarin orange), even a tropical element like fresh pineapple. By and large, despite what some producers intend, they are not particularly susceptible to improvement in the bottle, other than an allowance for the softening of youthful acids. Most will never be better than they are at one or two years old, and may already be beginning to taste a little tired at not much more than three. Drink young and fresh.

In the Pacific Northwest, Oregon Chardonnay tends to be crisper and slightly more austere on the palate than the wines of California, and the characteristic style is leaner, and less ostentatious as to fruit. Washington State has some fine Chardonnays, their erstwhile tendency to flabbiness having been overcome by some attractively balanced wines, though again with somewhat less fruit than California examples. Idaho has a more extreme climate, and tends to produce wines with high acidity, though they can be rounded out with gentle oak treatment.

Back east, New York State has a much cooler climate than the West Coast, and the Chardonnays it produces are in a correspondingly more bracing style, but the best wineries – notably on Long Island – are capitalizing on that to turn out some elegant and complex wines with ageing potential.

Chardonnay is also gaining in importance in Texas, where it makes a broad, immediately approachable style with plenty of ripe fruit.

Chardonnay ageing in new oak barrels (above). A lot of research has been carried out in the US to find out which oak best suits American Chardonnay, leading to a trend among certain producers away from French oak to native American oak.

Australia

Such was the soaring popularity of Australia's Chardonnays on external markets by the late 20th century that, at one stage, it began to look as if the country might not be able to produce enough to cope with the worldwide demand for them. One consequence is that there is now more Chardonnay planted across the country's vineyards than any other grape variety, white or red.

With the advent in the 1990s of the so-called flying winemakers – travelling wine consultants who flit between the hemispheres working as many vintages as they can fit into their schedules – the success of Australian wine had received the global endorsement that it was due.

Although it often involved a great swallowing of cultural pride on the part of the natives, the Australian itinerant winemakers were instrumental in revolutionizing winemaking practices in the viticultural backwaters of southern Europe. It was their skill with Chardonnay that, more than anything, served to create the demand for their services.

Australia taught the wine world that Chardonnay could be as unashamedly big and ripe and rich as you wanted it to be. Since the climate in most of the vineyard regions, the majority of which lie in the southeast of the country, is uniformly hot and dry, the fruit grown there regularly attains sky-high levels of natural sugar. Winemakers thus generally have to sharpen their wines up by controlled additions of tartaric acid to prevent them from tasting too sweet.

Nonetheless, the benchmark style of Aussie Chardonnay for years was a sunshine-yellow, extraordinarily luscious wine that, married with the vanilla and butterscotch flavours of new oak, was quite a way off being fully dry. High sugar means high alcohol (up to 14.5 per cent in some wines) so that, at the end of a generous glass, you certainly knew you'd had a drink.

As British and American wine consumers discovered an almost insatiable thirst for Australian Chardonnay, it became the habit in some critical quarters (myself included) to start calling into question whether these wines possessed true balance.

In latter years, trends in Chardonnay have begun to diversify in Australia, just as they have in California. There is a desire on the part of many winemakers, notably in the state of Western Australia, in South Australia's Coonawarra region, and in the Yarra Valley in Victoria, to make a subtler, more ageworthy (dare one say, more European?) style of Chardonnay, with better complexity.

At the top end of the quality ladder, there are some world-class wines. The problem, as so often, arises lower down the scale, where the unoaked Chardonnays in particular often seem to fighting to attain an elusive balance. Acidification is not always as finely judged as it might be, and where it isn't, a feeling of conflict with the obviously ripe fruit can be the result. Residual sugar levels are still often uncomfortably high, leading to wines that taste cloying after a glass, and are not best suited for accompanying food.

Much of Australia's wine is made from grapes sourced from different areas, blended to get the best balance of attributes in the final wine, so regional characteristics are proportionately less significant. However, an

Carpets of purple flowers surround Mountadam Estate (below) on the High Eden Ridge, in South Australia. Eden Valley, part of the Barossa Range, shares the soils and climate of the Barossa Valley, source of richly concentrated Chardonnays.

increasing number do bottle wines that are the produce of particular vineyard areas (the system of Geographical Indications, or GIs, is loosely and much less restrictively based on the European appellation approach), vinified separately so as to give a true expression of what the French would call their *terroir*.

In the state of South Australia, the Barossa Valley GI is one of the most important regions, producing broad-beamed, richly concentrated Chardonnays that make a dramatic impact on the palate. The McLaren Vale and Padthaway GIs are responsible for wines with perhaps a touch more finesse. Clare Valley is distinctly cooler, and its wines are correspondingly lighter and less upfront in style.

Chardonnays from the Goulburn Valley GI, Victoria, often possess hauntingly tropical fruit characters, while the cooler-climate Yarra Valley wines can resemble those of the less torrid parts of California. In Western Australia, the Margaret River GI is producing some unabashedly Burgundian wines that sometimes have that pungent whiff of green vegetable found on the Côte d'Or. For me, these are some of the most refined and attractive wines Australia has yet produced.

On the island of Tasmania, which constitutes its own GI, Chardonnay can be more austerely European still in its orientation, owing to the cool and fairly wet climate. Levels of grape acidity comparable to Chablis are not unheard of.

Stormy skies at first light (above) over the high ridges of the Barossa Range, South Australia.

New Zealand

(Above) Montana Estate, Marlborough, South Island. New Zealand Chardonnay is light, with juicily ripe fruit.

Chardonnay is New Zealand's second most widely planted white grape, behind Sauvignon Blanc. Grown in what is a considerably cooler and damper climate than Australia, the wines it produces tend, on the whole, to be noticeably lighter and more acidic.

That doesn't mean to say that Chardonnay lacks anything in terms of character because, in common with the even more fashionable Sauvignon, it nearly always possesses a positively unearthly degree of juicily ripe fruit. It is quite the norm to find pineapple and mango, grapefruit and apple, chasing each other around the glass, almost as though the grower had set out to confound the notion that Chardonnay isn't an aromatic variety.

About the richest styles come from the Gisborne and Poverty Bay regions on the eastern tip of the North Island, and these are the ones that respond best to oak-ageing. A little to the south, the wines of Hawkes Bay have more of a tang to them, and require a correspondingly more delicate touch with the wood.

Hopping over to the South Island, the climate becomes distinctly cooler still, and the typical Chardonnay style is snappier and more citric in Marlborough, and then quite taut and austere from Waipara and Central Otago.

South Africa

The lush green vineyards of Stellenbosch wineries Warwick Estate (above), and Thelema Vineyards (right), producers of rounded, golden Chardonnays. Coastal Stellenbosch is home to many of South Africa's finest producers.

When South Africa began to play a full part on the international wine scene in the early 1990s, many consumers were surprised to discover that Chardonnay was not the major force that it is elsewhere in the southern hemisphere. It played second fiddle to the much more widely planted Chenin Blanc. It still accounts for only a small percentage of vineyard land planted with white grapes, and what there is has been losing ground to Sauvignon Blanc.

Although South Africa remained largely isolated from world trade while the wine boom of the 1970s and 1980s was gathering momentum, it did profit in one respect. It was able to observe the trend for the heavily oaked, blockbuster style of Chardonnay (then inextricably associated with so-called New World winemaking) as it fell from favour among forward-looking winemakers, and simply sit it out.

How today's Chardonnays taste depends crucially on how far the vineyards lie from the southern coast. Those from further inland are grown in hotter conditions. So the Breede River Valley – over 96km (60 miles) from the cooling maritime influence of the Indian Ocean – is home to some of the Cape's biggest, burliest Chardonnays, while those from coastal Walker Bay are subtler, with the emphasis on fruit and more sharply defined acidity.

Rest of the World

SOUTH AMERICA

Chile's Chardonnays, as with its Cabernet Sauvignon wines, are made in two broad style categories. Some are made in a recognizably French vein, with pronounced acidity, light appley fruit and restrained oak maturation. Others go the whole hog, with full-blown charred oak flavours and a high-extract, alcoholic feel. It depends on the producer as much as the region. Argentina's wines, made largely in Mendoza in the foothills of the Andes, occupy a midway point between those two styles, with impressive balance and class.

EUROPE

Increasing concentrations of Chardonnay are cropping up across Italy now, from Aosta in the northwest all the way down to Puglia and Sicily, so that the variety is now the fourth most widely planted white grape. Although some rugged individualists are aiming for top-flight, barrel-fermented wines (and charging energetically for them), the basic style – best typified by the wines of the Alto Adige DOC on the Austrian border – are delicate, very lightly creamy wines made without recourse to wood.

Northern Spain is getting in on the act too, with plantings of Chardonnay vines in Penedés, Lérida, Somontano and Navarra, where it is often blended with local varieties such as Macabeo and Viura to make clean-cut, nutty, dry modern whites. It has achieved some significance in the production of the sparkling

Chardonnay is taking root in northern Italy, especially in Piedmont (above), in the foothills of the Alps, where it produces delicate, lightly creamy wines.

wine, cava, although many quality-conscious producers feel they can do without the reflected glory a non-Spanish variety appears to confer on the wines.

Chardonnay is of some modest importance in central Europe, particularly in Hungary, where the flying winemakers have been regular visitors. The wines tend to be made in the straightforward neutral style, clean and sharp for everyday drinking. When they do have some oak on them, it is only to add a gentler, rounder feel to them.

Further east, Bulgaria has been making Chardonnays since its heavily state-subsidised entry into western markets in the 1980s. A little on the clumsy side, they often didn't taste especially fresh, although the odd wine from Khan Krum in the east of the country could display a sort of sour-cream palatability.

There are also limited plantings in Slovenia and Romania but, among the other big western players, only Germany and Portugal managed largely to bypass the Chardonnay craze of the late 20th century.

Harvesting Chardonnay grapes (left) in Blatetz, Bulgaria. The quality of Chardonnay, one of many wines produced for the export market, varies, some of the best coming from Khan Krum.

CABERNET SAUVIGNON

Its pedigree is firmly founded in the gravelly soils of the Médoc, in the heart of Bordeaux. The king of red grapes, Cabernet Sauvignon has conquered vineyards across the world without losing the classic character that brought it such renown.

THE RED HALF of that hugely successful partnership that came to dominate international winemaking in the most recent generation is Cabernet Sauvignon. Alongside Chardonnay, it strode imperiously through the world's vineyards in the 1980s, often insisting that native varieties get out of its way wherever serious red wine was to be made. Although the example set before Cabernet growers – the classed-growth clarets of the Médoc in Bordeaux – is an illustrious one, it wasn't immediately easy to see why Cabernet came to be perceived as the pre-eminent red counterpart to the crowd-pleasing Chardonnay.

Its adaptablity to a variety of soils and climates is quite as impressive as that of Chardonnay, but its crop yield is more grudging, meaning that, even in the warmest climates, it has a heavy responsibility to earn its keep. Producers in regions with high climatic variation can often find that their higher-volume wines are basically subsidising the Cabernet.

As against that, Cabernet Sauvignon has suffered far less from the contempt induced by over-familiarity that has been Chardonnay's fate, for all that, among educated American consumers, ABC implicitly represents Anything but Cabernet as much as it stands for Anything but Chardonnay. There are three principal reasons for this.

Firstly, Cabernet comes in a much broader and more nuanced range of styles than Chardonnay. It isn't simply a question of deciding whether you want to make an unoaked, lightly oaked or very oaky wine. There are much finer gradations of style, and the grape is much less led by the nose when treated with oak than Chardonnay is.

Secondly, being a red wine, it is more often than not capable of developing with age. Just as the basic styles can be vastly different, so too the reactions of the wine to bottle maturation are excitingly divergent.

And thirdly, while it certainly conquered the known wine world quite as extensively as Chardonnay did, it somehow never became quite as axiomatically synonymous with red wine as Chardonnay did with white. Nobody ordering in a wine bar was ever heard asking for 'a glass of Cabernet' in the way that the fabled 'glass of Chardonnay' became the *lingua franca* of everyday white wine.

When on song, Cabernet Sauvignon wines deliver a heady rush of pure blackcurrant fruit, bolstered by density of texture and substantial ageing capacity, the sum of which seems to many wine-lovers the essence of all that is noble in a red wine. The greatest productions of the Médoc – Châteaux Lafite, Latour, Margaux, Mouton-Rothschild – are among the most famous names in wine, and if some of the class of those wines could be seen, however distantly, in a Cabernet Sauvignon from Chile, California or Australia, then the winemaker behind it might stand a fair chance of making the big time. (And so they have.)

Cabernet responds supremely well to oak-ageing, when the vanillin in new wood helps to soothe some of the natural acerbity of the young wine. That acerbity is basically tannin, that substance in youthful red wine that furs up the drinker's mouth, and which can obscure the fruit flavours. Cabernet is a thick-skinned variety, so its vinification results in naturally high tannin. Furthermore, its berries are relatively small compared to other red varieties, meaning that the proportion of tannin-bearing pip to flesh is higher.

What this means is that Cabernet producers need to make some finely detailed decisions in the winery about how to treat their wine. If you're selling to an audience that will kill for your next vintage, and expect to cellar the wine for upwards of a decade, you can spread your wings. If, on the other hand, your market positioning is about quick turnover from the winery to the retail industry, a great unwieldy slew of indigestible tannin is going to be box-office poison. And how much youthful fruit is too much for today's palates?

The small, dusty-blue Cabernet Sauvignon grape (right) produces wines of good tannin, body and aroma. It adapts easily to differing soils and climates, and in its finest form, with warm, late summer sun to ripen it fully, Cabernet creates complex, deeply coloured reds, packed with juicy blackcurrant fruit.

FRENCH ORIGINS

Bordeaux, specifically the left bank of the river Gironde, from the north of the Médoc down to the Graves. (On the right bank, it tends to play second fiddle to Merlot.)

WHERE ELSE IS IT GROWN?

Just about everywhere, although it has not made significant inroads into the cooler climates of northern Europe.

TASTING NOTES

In warm climates, almost any of the purple-skinned fruits – classically blackcurrants (perhaps most startlingly so in the best wines of Chile), but also black plums, brambles, damsons, etc. Often has a distinct note of fresh mint or even eucalyptus, especially in parts of Australia and Chile. Cooler climates can create a whiff of bitterness in it, often uncannily like chopped green pepper. Oak treatments generally emphasize a mineral austerity in the wine, likened in Bordeaux to the smell of cigar-boxes, cedarwood or – most recognizably – pencil shavings. With several years' bottle-age, it can take on aromas such as well-hung game, plum tomatoes, warm leather, dark chocolate, even soft Indian spices like cardamom, while the primary fruit begins to taste more like preserved fruit.

It's partly those considerations that have led to the realization that Cabernet Sauvignon is often much better-behaved in company. The original Bordeaux model is about blending in any case, and even a modest admixture of one or two other grapes can negotiate the toughness and brutality out of young Cabernet. Enter Merlot, Cabernet Franc and others in Bordeaux. Hello Shiraz in Australia.

Whatever the blend, the holy grail is a wine capable of acquiring complexity through long cellaring. Cabernets and Cabernet-based blends evolve in fascinatingly various ways as they age, depending on the quality of the primary fruit, the type of wood used for maturation, duration in the cask, and the length of time the wine spends in the bottle before you open it. Even in quite advanced old age, the telltale mineral purity of Cabernet Sauvignon still shines invitingly through.

Lighter styles of Cabernet are made in regions such as northern Italy and New Zealand, and many of these rub along quite well without oak. Indeed, when the wine is fully ripe and made from low-yielding vines, it can often be quite difficult to tell whether it has any oak on it or not. It can also, in common with others of the more assertive red varieties, make an attractive, full-flavoured rosé.

It is this potential for gathering complexity, though, that explains the high prices consistently paid for top Cabernets around the world. And that in turn is why so many winemakers take such enormous pains with it, when they may well be able to turn a faster buck growing something more mundane.

Bordeaux

A landmark in the Pauillac vineyards of first growth Château Latour (above), one of the five great premier cru châteaux of the Médoc.

The chai *at Château Mouton-Rothschild, Pauillac (below). The four famous communes of the Médoc – St-Estèphe, St-Julien, Margaux and Pauillac – are where the reputation of red Bordeaux is founded.*

Although Cabernet Sauvignon occupies far less vineyard land in Bordeaux than its traditional blending partner Merlot, it is nonetheless widely considered the pre-eminent grape variety in the region. This is because it plays a major part in the wines on which the reputation of Bordeaux is primarily founded – the *crus classés*, or classed growths, of the Médoc and Graves. When the region's classification system was drawn up in 1855, it was not that the judges ignored the Merlot-based wines of Pomerol and St-Emilion on the right bank; they simply didn't think they were in the same class.

That classification (outlined in detail in the chapter on Bordeaux) is now considered seriously outdated by many commentators, but the general perception that the majority of Bordeaux's most illustrious wines derive the greater part of their authority from the presence of Cabernet Sauvignon has never really changed, Pomerol notwithstanding.

Cabernet equips the young wine with those austere tannins that give it the structure it needs to age well, its pigment-rich skins endowing the wine with full-blooded depth of colour too. When claret-lovers refer to their favourite wine as having a profoundly serious quality that appeals as much to the intellect as it does to the senses, it is essentially Cabernet Sauvignon they have to thank for it.

If Cabernet enjoys such an exalted status, you may ask why more châteaux don't simply produce an unblended Cabernet wine, instead of making it share the bottle with Merlot and other varieties. The answer is partly that the grape works better in a team. Solo Cabernet, as some winemakers in California have found, is not necessarily an unalloyed blessing. In hot years, it can be just too much of a good thing, the resulting wines having colossal density and concentration, but not really seeming as though they are going to be ready to drink this side of the next appearance of Halley's comet.

The other reason for blending in Bordeaux is that, even though its southerly position makes this one of the warmest of France's classic regions, the summers are still highly variable. In problem vintages (such as the region endured through most of the 1970s, in 1980, 1984, during much of the early 1990s, and in 2002), Cabernet Sauvignon is the grape that suffers most. If the late summer is cool – and, what's worse, wet – it simply doesn't ripen properly, resulting in those vegetal, green-pepper tastes that make for harsh, depressing wine.

Since Merlot has much better tolerance for less-than-perfect vintage conditions, it makes sense for the growers to have the option of blending in some of the lighter Merlot to soften an overly astringent or green-tasting Cabernet.

In the great vintages, however, such as 2000, 2005 and 2009, the richness and power of Cabernet are worth celebrating, and the Merlot will only play a discreet supporting role, just smoothing the edges a little, so that the full glory of ripe Cabernet can be shown to maximum advantage.

Most of the wines that occupy the five ranks of the 1855 hierarchy come from four vineyard areas to the west of the river Gironde: St-Estèphe, Pauillac, St-Julien and Margaux. From top to bottom, collectively, they extend over not much more than 40km (25 miles), but there are subtle differences in the styles of Cabernet-based wine they produce.

St-Estèphe generally makes the fiercest wine, with typically tough tannins that take years to fall away, and a very austere aroma that is often compared to fresh tobacco. Pauillac – the commune that boasts three of the five first growths in Lafite, Latour and Mouton-Rothschild – is a little less severe, even when young. Its wines have more emphatic blackcurrant fruit than those of St-Estèphe, and a seemingly more complicated pot-pourri of spice and wood notes as they age.

St-Julien, which adjoins Pauillac, exhibits many of the characteristics of its neighbour, although its wines somehow display a softer fruit – more like dark plums and blackberries than blackcurrants – as they begin to mature. The best wines of Margaux are noted for their extravagant perfume, although in general the

underlying wine is lighter than anything from further north, the exception being first-growth Château Margaux itself.

South of the city of Bordeaux, the large area of the Graves makes wines that vary in character. These range from relative featherweights that constitute some of the region's lightest reds, to those that have a mineral earthiness to them, thought to derive from the gravelly soils that give this part of Bordeaux its name. Elsewhere, the quality becomes gradually more prosaic until, at the lowest level of AC Bordeaux, the bulk of the produce is hard red jug-wine of no obvious appeal.

In Bordeaux, it is the name of the property rather than the producer that goes on the label. Much time and attention is devoted to studying the relative form and fitness of the most famous estates as each new vintage appears on the market. Those planning to buy even a single bottle of top-flight Bordeaux would do well to consider the present reputation of a château as well as the quality of the vintage.

Cabernet Sauvignon vines (above) planted in the poor, gravelly soils of St-Estèphe, in the Médoc, on the right bank of the Gironde river.

United States

Cabernet Sauvignon was introduced to California in the 19th century in the form of cuttings from Bordeaux. The readiness with which it took to the fertile soils in which it was planted is evidenced by the fact that it already had something of a reputation among the American wine cognoscenti before that century was out. The best was held to come from the Napa Valley, north of San Francisco, where the late hot summers resulted in strapping great wines of swarthy hue, thickly textured, and capable of delivering a hefty alcoholic blow to the unsuspecting drinker.

Some might facetiously say that not much has changed. Certainly, in many consumers' minds, the benchmark style of California Cabernet has been fiercely tannic, often virtually black wines that potentially took a decade or two to unravel into a state of anything like drinkability. It would be grossly simplistic to characterize all California Cabernets in that way today, but it was undeniably the predominant style of the wine in the 1970s and 1980s, and there are certainly some wineries that still nail their colours to that particular mast.

The tower in the vineyard at Silver Oak Cellars, Napa Valley (below).

Moreover, it is not as though there aren't perfectly good antecedents for it. Most classed-growth Bordeaux in the hot years like 2003 and 2005 would answer that description – or something very like it – when first released. The wines are not intended to be drunk straight away in any case. Château Latour is after all still black as sin and guarded by snarling tannins at ten years old. It's almost as though a dose of old-world condescension were at work here: it's fine for the Bordelais, but really doesn't suit you.

The problem lay in the fact that not many consumers are attuned to drinking wine that tastes so forbidding, even if they can readily afford the prices commanded by it. Producers realized a middle way had to be found between budding West Coast Latours and insipid commercial jug-wine.

What happened from the 1970s on was a huge upsurge in experimental plantings of Cabernet Sauvignon across the state of California, as growers set out to find the optimum microclimates for the variety. Experiments, by their nature, can produce failures, and where the

Picking Cabernet Sauvignon grapes in vineyards south of Prosser, Washington State (left). Despite the fairly cool climate, some fine Cabernets have been made in the Pacific Northwest.

A vineyard worker harvesting Cabernet Sauvignon grapes in Calistoga, California (above).

grape was grown in cooler areas, the outcome was wines that had more than a touch of the familiar green bell pepper/asparagus vegetal quality that Cabernet is prone to when it lacks sufficient ripening time. Oak maturation was sometimes excessive too, giving wines with an exaggeratedly woody taste.

Without a doubt, however, California – the Napa Valley in particular – has also turned out some wonderfully sleek, opulently fruit-filled Cabernets of world-class status, many of them blended with others of the Bordeaux varieties (these blends sometimes given the label Meritage).

In the Pacific Northwest, the climate is generally a little too cool for producing great Cabernets, although Washington State has come up with some fine examples. The tendency is to compensate for less than generous fruit flavours by applying fairly heavy oak maturation, which runs the risk of creating top-heavy wines. Oregon indeed is a much safer bet for cool-ripening Pinot Noir than sun-seeking Cabernet.

Texas, on the other hand, is proving to be highly Cabernet-friendly, and the grape is now the most widely planted red variety there, having expanded rapidly over the last 20 years. The state style is one of big, rich, upfront fruit, some savoury herb characters and good weight, but with tannins kept in check. In time, this could emerge as the best American Cabernet territory outside the Napa Valley. Virginia too is producing some distinguished Cabernets.

Australia

Australia's approach to Cabernet Sauvignon, its second most planted red grape after Shiraz, has been much less conflicted than than of California. The aim among its growers is all about emphasizing the kind of ripe juicy drinkability that wins friends even among those who don't consider themselves fans of rich red wine. In the ultra-reliable climates enjoyed by most of Australia's wine-growing regions, Cabernet more often than not attains levels of ripeness Bordeaux's producers would give their eye-teeth for.

Oak barrel ageing is used enthusiastically by the great majority of Cabernet growers. When your wine is as rich and dense and blackcurranty as much Australian Cabernet is, you can afford to be generous with the oak treatment. At the same time, however, the classic style aims to maximize fruit characters without extracting too much tannin from the grapeskins. Thus, although it is an intensely concentrated wine, it doesn't necessarily scour your mouth with harsh astringency when it's young.

The chances are that, even if you are unfamiliar with the producer, a Cabernet from practically anywhere in Australia will deliver plump, soft, cassis-scented wine with an enagaging creamy texture and no hard edges. That is not to say that there aren't wineries intent on producing more austere Cabernets in a style built to age, but even these tend to come round far sooner than most California Cabernets, or Cabernet-based clarets, made in the same idiom. Even tasted in their infancy, the tannins on Australian wines such as these are nowhere near as severe as the colour may lead you to expect.

Blending is widely practised for Cabernet here too, with Shiraz having been its best bottle-friend since the 1960s, a recipe that Australia taught the world.

Australia's Cabernet pioneer was one John Riddoch (honoured in the name of one of the country's best classic Cabernets), who first planted the variety in the last decade of the 19th century in a part of South Australia called Coonawarra. Coonawarra's chief distinguishing characteristic is a narrow strip of red soil the colour of paprika, known as *terra rossa*. And it is here that Cabernet Sauvignon still produces its most gorgeously distinctive performances in Australia, and some of the world's best.

Endless rows of Cabernet Sauvignon vines under an endless Australian sky (below), in Clare Valley, South Australia. The hotter, drier climate encourages rich, dense Cabernets.

Coonawarra wines often have a chocolatey richness to them, tinged with hints of mocha coffee beans. Some, noting the relatively cooler climate the region enjoys, have compared it to a southern-hemisphere Bordeaux, but Coonawarra stands in no need of such vicarious honour. Its wines are nothing like claret; they have their own uniquely spicy style.

South Australia is the most important state overall for Cabernet wines. In the heat of the Barossa Valley GI, they tend to be richly coloured and thickly textured, with an intensity like preserved fruits. From McLaren Vale, the wines are often more delicately proportioned, with slightly higher acid levels. In the Eden Valley, Cabernets of almost European profile are being produced, with aromatic spice notes in them, and often a dash of mint.

Coonawarra takes that spice component a little further, and there is sometimes a fugitive hint of something exotically pungent, like Worcester sauce. Riverland is a much less distinguished bulk-producing region, where the wines are made in an easy-drinking, uncomplicated style.

Victoria makes Cabernet in the leaner, mintier manner. The vineyards are mainly located in the centre of the state, especially in the fashionable region of Bendigo. Despite its notably cool climate, Yarra Valley has been responsible for some of Australia's most extraordinarily intense Cabernets, with astonishing depth.

Cabernets from the Margaret River GI in Western Australia tend to the hauntingly scented end of the spectrum, with particularly defined acidity and consequently good ageing potential.

Tasmania's cool, damp climate is better suited to other varieties, but there have been successes with lighter, more sharply angled Cabernets than are found on the mainland.

The famous terra rossa *soil of Coonawarra, South Australia (above). Vineyard land here is highly prized for the quality of grapes it yields.*

Other Non-European

SOUTH AFRICA

Cabernet Sauvignon became, in the early 1990s, the most widely planted red grape variety in South Africa. Early efforts were often discouraging, partly as a result of Cabernet being grown in sites that were either too cool or too hot for it, and partly because the specific variant of the grape widely grown in Cape vineyards wasn't of the best quality. The results were often wines that lacked convincing fruit definition.

All that has changed in recent years, with new clones of the grape yielding riper, richer fruit flavours, and growers allowing them full ripening time on the vine. Coastal Stellenbosch, Franschhoek, and inland Paarl have turned out to be the most promising regions, with many convincingly classy, ageworthy wines emerging. Wines made according to the Bordeaux recipe, using Cabernet Franc and Merlot to soften some

of Cabernet Sauvignon's severity, have been the best, but blends with Shiraz can be juicily appealing too in their way.

CHILE

During the course of the 1980s, Chile was the southern-hemisphere epicentre for European wine consultants, and no variety was more consulted on than Cabernet Sauvignon. When no less an eminence than Gilbert Rokvam of Château Lafite arrived at the Los Vascos winery in Colchagua, it seemed pretty clear that Chile had made its entrance on the world wine map with due fanfare, at least as far as Cabernet was concerned. Early results were amazing.

What has happened since is that Chilean Cabernet has diverged into two broadly identifiable styles. One is what Europeans tend to think of as the benchmark New World idiom, ripely blackcurranty Cabernet of sumptuous, velvety texture, with low tannins and plenty of oak. There are numerous examples of this style and, while they all benefit from a couple of years' ageing, they can be enjoyed relatively young, at barely more than a year old.

The other style is much more austere, cedary wine of high acidity and more pronounced tannins, vinified in a way that is intended to help it to age in the bottle, and owing much to the taste of classic Médoc claret. Wines from the Maipo, Rapel and Casablanca regions have registered some stunning successes in this style.

At its best, Chilean Cabernet Sauvignon can display scents of the most intensely pure essence of blackcurrant to be found in any Cabernet produced anywhere. They may taste a little one-dimensional at first, but they broaden and deepen with age into something altogether thrilling. The wines made in the French style are the longest-lived, with older vintages taking on the savoury complexity of fine mature Médoc.

ARGENTINA

On the other side of the Andes, the Mendoza province of Argentina is now showing its own potential as a major runner in the Cabernet stakes. Strangely enough, the grape has had to play understudy in the vineyards to Malbec, one of the bit-part players in red Bordeaux (blending the two is widely practised), but plantings are steadily on the increase.

The towering Drakensteinberg mountains form a stunning backdrop to the higher and cooler district of Franschhoek in coastal Stellenbosch, South Africa (below), source of classy Cabernets capable of ageing.

Initially, varietal Cabernets were rather sternly tannic, and dominated by wood flavours rather than fruit, on account of their having been aged too long in old oak casks. Outside investment was slower to arrive in Argentina than it was in Chile, and so the wines, Cabernet in particular, took a little longer to settle into their best style.

Cabernet is now being made in a generally French-oriented manner, from plantings in high-altitude vineyards to mitigate some of the formidable heat of the growing season. Expect rich plum and cassis fruit, backed by savoury herb flavours and a judicious amount of tannin.

High-altitude sites in Argentina's second biggest region, San Juan, look equally promising for Cabernet.

NEW ZEALAND

Most of New Zealand's vineyard land has proved to be too cool and damp for Cabernet, which is notoriously bad-tempered if it doesn't get enough sun. Some varietal Cabernet has that telltale green pepper flavour, with high acidity, though low tannin. Painstaking site selection has, however, produced some encouraging successes on the North Island, particularly in the Hawkes Bay area, and from Waiheke Island near Auckland.

As elsewhere, blending is the key, and the Cabernet-Merlot partnership has emerged as a surefire winner for many growers. There are now some very attractive wines of real complexity and depth, in a midweight style not a million miles from the softer wines of Bordeaux, though quicker to mature.

Harvesting Cabernet Sauvignon at Los Vascos (above) in the hot Colchagua Valley, Rapel, Chile. Los Vascos produces Cabernets moulded in the classic Médoc style.

Old Cabernet Sauvignon vines owned by the grand 19th-century bodega, Cousiño Macul (left), in Maipo, Chile. The vines date back to the 1930s.

Other European

Pickers on the Marqués de Griñón's estate near Toledo, in the hot centre of Spain (above). The estate has drawn attention for its structured, long-ageing Cabernets.

The Torres Mas la Plana vineyard in Penedés, planted solely with Cabernet vines (below). Torres and Jean León set a precedent for Cabernet in Spain in the '60s.

FRANCE

Just outside Bordeaux, in appellations such as Bergerac and Buzet, the permitted grape varieties are the same as in Bordeaux itself, and from certain producers, the wines can rival everyday claret. Cabernet Sauvignon has made major inroads into the Languedoc-Roussillon, in France's warm southern zone, where it most often appears as varietal Vin de Pays d'Oc. A small amount is also grown in the Loire as blending material with Gamay, or as a minor component in sparkling rosés.

SPAIN AND PORTUGAL

Cabernet Sauvignon established a bridgehead on the Iberian peninsula when it was planted in Penedés by the Torres family and Jean León in the 1960s. Varietal Cabernets from that region, from Castile and the Montes de Toledo are often made in the opaquely concentrated, monumental style for long keeping.

Many producers, in regions such as Ribera del Duero and Costers del Segre, have developed blends of Cabernet Sauvignon with Spain's indigenous superstar grape Tempranillo, often with exciting results.

The same inclination towards blended wines has tended to be followed by those Portuguese growers who have planted Cabernet, although there are some accomplished varietal wines produced on the Setúbal peninsula south of

Lisbon. Otherwise, the grape has become an important blending ingredient for many growers in the Douro and Alentejo regions.

ITALY

Italy's growers have always been a little cavalier, particularly in the northern regions, in distinguishing Cabernet Sauvignon from its Bordeaux sibling Cabernet Franc. Thus a Trentino wine labelled Cabernet may be one or the other, or both. Yet the two grapes are in reality quite distinct, and produce different styles of wine.

Less confusion arises in Tuscany, where Cabernet Sauvignon is allowed to make up a minor part of the blend in Chianti, and in lesser-known reds such as Carmignano. A revolution in Italian wine was effected in the 1970s by a group of Tuscan innovators, led by the highly respected family house of Antinori. They began working outside the Italian DOC regulations to produce towering reds that made free use of Cabernet Sauvignon, either blended with the Chianti grape Sangiovese, or the other Bordeaux varieties. Eventually, these wines were brought into either the Bolgheri DOC or the wider regional IGT designation for Tuscany.

Cabernet has also gained a foothold in Piedmont in the northwest, where it is often bottled either wholly or almost unblended in the Langhe DOC.

CENTRAL AND EASTERN EUROPE

The cheap red wine boom in the 1970s and 1980s was sustained almost single-handedly by the state-subsidised exports of Bulgaria. For a supposedly marginal winemaking climate, Bulgarian Cabernets generally offered the sorts of easily lovable, softly plummy fruit flavours that producers of less expensive Bordeaux could only dream about. The wines were smoothed with plenty of oak, and were often released as Reserve bottlings after several years' ageing in the state cellars.

At their best, these wines managed to combine enough depth of character to grace a serious dinner table with the kind of instant drinkability that made them surefire party wines. Sadly, the breakup of the old communist state monopoly immediately resulted in wild inconsistencies in quality but, with gathering private investment, Bulgaria is gradually coming back into contention.

Hungary, Moldova and Romania are all capable of producing good Cabernet at a price the wine-drinker wants to pay. Hungary's Villany and Romania's Dealul Mare are among the most propitious regions.

Other Cabernet-based one-offs include the legendary Château Musar of Lebanon, a blend of Cabernet with Cinsault and Carignan made in the Bekaa Valley by the indefatigable Serge Hochar. Where other growers worry about problems like spring frost, the Bekaa has been more prone to war, invasion and rocket attacks. That the fruit of Hochar's labours is a magnificently long-lived and powerful wine is a due tribute to his indomitability.

Greek Cabernet Sauvignon may one day be a force to be reckoned with, if varietal and blended bottlings from areas such as the Atalanti Valley in central Greece, and the Côtes de Meliton in Sithonia in the north, are anything to go by.

Bulgaria's vineyards, like these overlooking the village of Ustina, near Plovdiv (above), were the source of much commercially successful Cabernet in the 1980s.

SAUVIGNON BLANC

The grape of the famous Loire whites, Sancerre and Pouilly-Fumé, Sauvignon also brought New Zealand to the attention of the wine world, with a fruit cocktail of a wine that proved the versatility of this variety.

THE PREDOMINANT shift in consumer tastes in white wine in the last decade or so has been the transfer of allegiance from Chardonnay to Sauvignon Blanc. In many ways, it's easy to see why. The two grapes' characteristics are diametrically opposed. Whereas Chardonnay was typically seen as a golden, fat-textured, buttery white wine that owed much of its identity to the influence of wood, Sauvignon is a pale, relatively light and acidic wine nearly always vinified without oak and endowed with a piercingly distinct perfume. In other words, when Chardonnay fatigue began to set in, here was the antidote.

A well-made Sauvignon performs its role as light refreshment almost too well. The simplicity of this style has led some in the wine commentariat to treat the grape with mild contempt. This undoubtedly does it a great injustice; it is in fact capable of impressive complexity. Sauvignon is responsible for two of France's most celebrated dry white wines – Sancerre and Pouilly-Fumé, stylistically inimitable stars of the Loire. And when the vine's yields are controlled, it can display a wealth of uninihibited ripe fruit, as shown by the roaring success of New Zealand Sauvignon.

In addition to its upfront fruit, Sauvignon grown on certain flinty soils of the upper Loire valley in the centre of France can take on an inexplicable, but oddly powerful, smoky quality that deceives many into thinking it must have had some oak treatment. At its most pungent, it can resemble the savoury fume of woodsmoke; in a gentler vein, it may remind you of the wisps of steam from an espresso machine. This attribute is celebrated in the suffix of the name of Pouilly-Fumé, and it came to be much imitated in the California of the 1970s and 1980s, after Napa Valley winemaker Robert Mondavi renamed his Sauvignon wine Fumé Blanc. Sometimes the elusive smokiness was there; quite often one searched in vain.

Styles in Sauvignon have been subject to wide international vicissitudes in the last 20 years. Some Fumé Blanc was given time in oak, as a way of imitating the flint-derived smokiness of the upper Loire wines. Many California growers, though, have resorted to bottling the wine with relatively high residual sugar, as a way of mitigating its acidity and masking its herbaceous pungency. But if they

The green Sauvignon Blanc grape (right), here in Pessac-Léognan where it is destined for blending with Sémillon for the dry white Bordeaux. A prolific vine, but when yields are controlled it is capable of massive fruit character.

feel it needs such cosmetic disguising, why grow it at all? Even now, Sauvignon is often California's weakest shot.

In Bordeaux, where it was traditionally blended with Sémillon (see page 62) for both dry and sweet whites, it has begun to take centre-stage as a solo performer in the dry wines. Plantings have increased to reflect the worldwide modishness of the grape, and there are some intriguing flavours being coaxed out of it, pineapple as well as gooseberry.

More than any other region outside France, though, it is New Zealand that helped to establish the international status of Sauvignon. It may very well be that, across the board, New Zealand's winemakers now have a better understanding of the grape than the French. Wines from Marlborough in particular offer more ecstatically happy fruit flavour per mouthful than practically any other dry whites in the world. For every trend, however, there's a backlash, and in the last few years, I've begun to detect a slight fatigue among consumers with the thorough-going juicy-fruit style of Marlborough Sauvignon.

In general, Sauvignon is lost without a healthy measure of good crisp acidity, which is why, in very hot areas, it can result in a rather flabby and fruitless wine. It's important to remember that Sauvignon is not meant to be a neutral-tasting glass of nothing-in-particular. We've got Pinot Grigio for that.

FRENCH ORIGINS

Bordeaux, where it is nearly always blended with Sémillon (and perhaps a drop of Muscadelle). The upper Loire valley is where France's top varietal Sauvignons are based, and less exalted wines are made further west along the Loire in Touraine.

WHERE ELSE IS IT GROWN?

Fairly widespread, but particularly important in New Zealand, Chile and South Africa, less so in the United States and Australia. Increasing plantings in the warmer Languedoc and northern Spain have proved surprisingly successful.

TASTING NOTES

Practically the whole gamut of fruit flavours, ranging from sour green fruits like gooseberry and tart apple or pear to astonishingly exotic notes such as Charentais melon, passion fruit and mango. It very often has a precise nose of blackcurrants. Vegetable flavours can loom large too. Green peas, asparagus and sweet red (bell) peppers often crop up in New Zealand examples. Then there is a curiously pungent animal quality in many cool-climate, especially Loire, versions that is often compared to cat's pee, or even to male sweat. If you're lucky, that fugitive wisp of faintly acrid smoke is there as well.

France

Early-morning mist (above) over Sauvignon vines in the Loire's famous Pouilly-Fumé appellation.

LOIRE

In the vineyards around the upper reaches of the river Loire, in the centre of France, unblended Sauvignon Blanc reigns supreme. It wasn't that long ago that these crisp, scented dry white wines, designed to be drunk within a couple of years of harvest, were not especially highly regarded even within France itself. As fashion has shifted away from richer and oakier styles of white, Loire Sauvignon – Sancerre in particular – has found itself catapulted to the height of popularity.

Pouilly-Fumé and Sancerre are the two most famous appellations for Sauvignon. They are situated on opposite sides of the river, on the east and west banks respectively. It is a very accomplished taster indeed who can spot one from the other when, at their best, they both capture the combination of refreshing green fruit flavours, snappy acids and distant smoky aromas that typify the grape in these parts.

The fashionability of the wines has elevated their prices, which – at the generic supermarket own-brand end of the quality spectrum – have become all but unpalatable, given the fact that there is nothing particularly expensive about their production. As well as that, there is the uncomfortable fact that, in Pouilly-Fumé particularly, there are too many indifferent producers making unfocused wines from the product of overcropping vines.

To the west of Sancerre are three less well-known Sauvignon appellations. They offer most of the flavour of the wines of their more exalted neighbours at generally kinder prices. The best, and closest to Sancerre, is Menetou-Salon. Further west, across the river Cher, Quincy and Reuilly produce brisk, assertive Sauvignons in a clean but slightly less concentrated style than the others.

In the heartland of the Loire region, the Touraine district – more famous for its Chenin Blanc wines – also has a lot of Sauvignon. A fair amount of it gets used as blending fodder, but some varietal wines are bottled under the label Touraine Sauvignon. In good years, they too can offer a glass of cheerfully fruity white, increasingly showing something of the intensity of the wines of the upper Loire.

The village of Sancerre (right) that gives the appellation its name stands on a hilltop close to the river Loire, overlooking the vineyards.

BORDEAUX

The dry white wines of Bordeaux were taken by the scruff of the neck and marched into the modern world during the 1980s. Too often stale and dispiriting creations based on over-produced Sémillon prior to that, they have benefited hugely from the trend towards cooler fermentations in temperature-controlled stainless steel.

As Sauvignon wines from further north gained in modishness and therefore retail value, it dawned on the Bordelais that perhaps they could play a part in the Sauvignon craze by vinifying more of what was after all one of their own main grapes. The percentage of Sauvignon in many of the blends has accordingly sharply increased, bringing in its train a greater freshness and zip to the wines.

Top of the quality tree is the region of Pessac-Léognan at the northern end of the Graves, where a healthy scattering of wines from properties such as Domaine de Chevalier, and Châteaux Haut-Brion and Laville-Haut-Brion, have always shown true class. Some producers, such as Couhins-Lurton, use only Sauvignon in their whites. The smart operators have also employed barrel-ageing (and even fermentation in oak too) in order to achieve a rich, tropical-fruit style that is far more opulent than the unoaked Sauvignons of the Loire.

The large production of the Entre-Deux-Mers region is generally more humble stuff, although the best of even these are beginning to shine, and there are producers turning out oaked, unblended Sauvignon to rival the best of Pessac-Léognan. Sauvignon also plays a supporting role in the great sweet wines of Bordeaux, to lend a flash of balancing acid to the noble-rotted Sémillon.

ELSEWHERE

The Bergerac appellation on the river Dordogne has the same grape varieties as Bordeaux, and can turn out some light, refreshing Sauvignon-based blends, as can the Côtes de Duras to the south. White wines labelled Vin de Pays des Côtes de Gascogne, from further down in southwest France, may be made from any of a number of grapes, and there is a smattering of varietal Sauvignon among them.

Although it may seem inauspiciously hot, the increased plantings of Sauvignon in the Languedoc are yielding some attractively crisp, fruity Vins de Pays d'Oc that owe their super-fresh quality to cold fermentation in stainless steel. Choice of the right harvest-time is all. That, and controlling the vigour of the vines so they don't over-produce.

Finally, there is a lone outpost of Sauvignon in the far north of what is technically the Burgundy region, near Chablis. Sauvignon de St-Bris is an historical oddity, best described as tasting like Sauvignon made in the style of Chardonnay, with the recognizable green fruit but with smoother contours than are found in the Loire versions. (Some Chablis growers also possess vineyard land here.) The wines were promoted to the full AOC designation in 2003.

In the Sauternes region, as here at Château Suduiraut (below), Sauvignon Blanc brings a streak of fresh acidity to balance the sweetness of noble-rotted Sémillon.

New Zealand

Sauvignon Blanc devotees weaned on the exhilarating flavours of New Zealand's finest efforts won't be surprised to learn that it is now the country's most extensively planted white variety, recently overtaking Chardonnay in acres of vineyard. The grape shot to prominence here in the 1980s on the back of the wine made by the bulk-producing Montana winery in Marlborough on the South Island. The commercial success of its Sauvignon – never less than a harvest festival of pure raw-fruit ripeness – was founded on its sheer exuberance of flavour, and shored up for many years by the fact that its export price hardly moved. And that despite the fact that few wines have further to travel to the international marketplace than those of southern New Zealand.

Having sparked a trend, Montana's example was quickly followed by a host of other wineries. That surge of abundant fruit is present in nearly all the wines of the Marlborough region, although occasionally the acidity can be out of focus, or – as in the troubled vintages of 2003 and 2008 – just a little too aggressive. There has been a distinct tendency among some producers to aim for more Loire-like levels of acidity, which has resulted in wines that have some of the flintiness of their French counterparts, and correspondingly less obvious fruit. Blending with Semillon can achieve a textural depth and lushness in certain wines.

Adjacent to Marlborough, the South Island region of Nelson makes some sharply defined, cool-climate Sauvignons in the nettly, herbaceous style.

The slightly softer style of Sauvignon really comes into its own in the North Island region of Hawkes Bay. The fruit here seems less green and more peachy, and there is a concomitantly greater readiness to use a little oak in the vinification, though by no means universally. These can be very attractive wines.

The Cloudy Bay winery in New Zealand's Marlborough district (below), one of the country's greatest success stories with the Sauvignon grape.

Other Regions

SOUTH AFRICA

As elsewhere, it's the cooler areas that do best with Sauvignon Blanc in South Africa, and there are now some brilliantly aromatic, concentrated wines being produced. Most of the premium examples are made in the acerbically dry, smoky style of the Loire, with some even recalling the flintiness of good Pouilly-Fumé. The fruit characters of the wines tend to the green, sappy end of the scale, but there is the odd one with something like the fruit-basket juiciness of the textbook New Zealand style. Walker Bay, Elgin, Durbanville and the cooler parts of Stellenbosch have been the best regions for Sauvignon.

SOUTH AMERICA

There was a large, and for some time intractable, problem with Sauvignon Blanc in Chile, which was that a lot of it wasn't. Quite a few growers had a grape called Sauvignonasse, thinking it was the Loire variety, whereas it was in fact the dull, neutral-tasting relative of a grape native to northeast Italy. Chilean Sauvignon, however, can now be bought with confidence, with most wines representing a gentler version of the crisp Loire style. Wines from the cooler Casablanca region are a good bet.

Astonishingly well-defined Sauvignons with tropical fruit, sharply etched acids and a touch of smoke are being made in Argentina's high-volume Mendoza province.

AUSTRALIA

The hotter the wine region, the less likely it is to be capable of producing the appetizing fruit and natural crispness that Sauvignon wines need. Many of Australia's efforts have traditionally been hampered by a lack of sharp definition. Not unexpectedly, the cooler Margaret River GI in Western Australia has proved the most propitious, with some refreshing, sappy wines.

UNITED STATES

The Mondavi winery's attempt to elevate the status of California Sauvignon by renaming it Fumé Blanc didn't manage to persuade many other growers to take the variety to their hearts. If they have Sauvignon at all, they often try to disguise what they see as a troubling pungency in the flavour of the grape by ageing in oak, or else leaving a distracting quantity of residual sugar in the wine. Washington State is very often a better source of fruit-driven, tangy Sauvignon for drinking young.

The Cullens winery in the Margaret River area of Western Australia (above) has consistently produced one of the country's more sharply defined Sauvignons.

Chile's cooler Casablanca Valley (left) is proving a good spot to grow characterful, fruity Sauvignon Blanc.

PINOT NOIR

Difficult to grow, difficult to vinify, but still producers across the globe are attracted to this temperamental grape variety, tempted to try matching the classic style of Burgundy's greatest red wines.

OF ALL THE French grape varieties that have migrated around the viticultural world, this is the one that excites the greatest passions. More tears are shed, greater energy expended, more hand-wringing despair engendered over it than over any other variety. It is not, by and large, an endeavour for those who relish a quiet life.

Pinot Noir is the only grape permitted in the great majority of red burgundies (the only exceptions being at or near the bottom end of the quality ladder). At the summit sit the *grand cru* wines of the region's most illustrious estates, wines of positively exotic complexity that offer a once-in-a-lifetime experience of dazzling opulence at a once-in-a-lifetime price. All the red-wine appellations of the Côte d'Or, however, are capable of producing great Pinot at one time or another – they don't call it the Slope of Gold for nothing.

So why all the heartbreak?

First off, it emphatically doesn't like being heat-stressed. Burgundy is cool and wet, prone to spring frosts and hail, to an extent that, even here in its ancestral home, it is profoundly vintage-dependent. It has been estimated that, on average, two years out of every three are inadequate for producing great wine (although climate change may gradually be lending its producers a helping hand for the time being).

In off-vintages, the result is a thin, bitter wine with no fruit to speak of, and a streak of hard, spiteful acid that acts as a powerful repellent in its youth. Pinots produced in these conditions are among the feeblest red wines in the fine wine sector, and the labour of love that has to be lavished on them accounts for that part of the sky-high asking prices that isn't accounted for by the region's reputation.

Early experiments with Pinot outside Europe too often fell into this trap. Plantings in the cooler areas of the United States and in New Zealand often combined scything acidity with chaotically high alcohol, while Australian

efforts grown in sweltering conditions were muddy, unfocused and clumsily smothered with extraneous oak.

So should we just draw a veil over Pinot Noir and move on to the next grape? Ah, no.

Grow it in the right climate, preferably in soils with some limestone in them (as in Burgundy), and protect it against the rash of diseases that its flesh is heir to, including rot if there is any rain at harvest-time, and the potential payoff is wine of uniquely haunting beauty, and extraordinary longevity.

Ripe, healthy bunches of Pinot Noir grapes (right). A thin-skinned grape that is highly sensitive to climate and soil, and notoriously difficult to nurture, Pinot Noir can make ripely fruity reds of great class. It is also invaluable in the production of sparkling wine.

It is a thin-skinned variety – physically as well as temperamentally – which means that it generally produces lighter, less forbiddingly tannic wines than Cabernet Sauvignon does. They are correspondingly approachable earlier in their development, although their naturally high acidity does need time to settle. Keep the most concentrated ones for a few years more, and their maturation is astonishing for such a comparatively light wine. An intense gaminess comes over them, something between well-hung meat and black truffle, and their initial red fruit deepens into the savoury scents of herbs and grilling meat.

Increasingly, since the 1990s, growers outside France have got the hang of Pinot Noir. In California (particularly Carneros) and Oregon, and in selected sites across New Zealand, fantastic results are being achieved. The wines often possess brighter, more resonant red fruit in their first flush than burgundy does (think raspberries and red cherries), but the savouriness is there too, and the acid profiles are such that they age majestically. They aren't necessarily much more affordable than mid-range burgundy, but you are appreciably getting your money's worth.

Additionally, Pinot Noir plays an important role in the production of champagne and other sparkling wines, where it adds depth and potential longevity to the Chardonnay, as well as colour to the rosés. Red Pinot wine adds scented charm to much pink champagne. It has enjoyed a highly successful entrée on to the Spanish cava scene, for example, where its delicacy compared to the traditional Spanish red grapes has made for some more graceful pink sparklers than was usually the norm.

FRENCH ORIGINS
Burgundy and Champagne. Also used in some of the light reds and rosés of the Loire, and the red wine of Alsace.

WHERE ELSE IS IT GROWN?
California, Oregon, Australia, New Zealand, Chile and South Africa. Quite important in central Europe – southern Germany, Switzerland, and points east – but still fairly rare along the Mediterranean. Anybody making sparkling wine by the traditional champagne method is likely to use some Pinot.

TASTING NOTES
In youth, it can possess light aromas of red fruits, typically raspberry, strawberry, redcurrant, cherry. In parts of California and Australia, it also has a faint note of coffee bean or mocha. Nearly always has an element of meatiness – beef stock in young wines, shading to well-hung game as it ages, overlaid in the very best with the other-worldly pungency of black truffle. Classically (or notoriously, depending on your tastes) mature wines can also display a distinctly rank smell, politely described as 'barnyardy', but really referring to what you might accidentally put your foot in as you walk through the barnyard.

France

Levelling Pinot Noir grapes in the traditional wooden press at Champagne Bollinger (above).

Harvested Pinot Noir grapes resting in traditional wicker baskets (below) at Louis Latour, in Aloxe-Corton on the Côte d'Or, the home of most of Burgundy's famous names.

Betting on vintage conditions in Burgundy as harvest-time approaches makes for slightly more peace of mind than playing Russian roulette – but only just. In most years, the region's white grape variety, Chardonnay, fares reasonably well: only torrential rain during the picking can really ruin it at the eleventh hour. Pinot Noir, the only runner in the red wine stakes, is a horse of another colour altogether.

At least until the late 1990s, it was possible to say that, more often than not, Pinot Noir yielded disappointing results. Precisely because out-and-out successes were so hard-won, great red burgundy came to be valued by many as the most precious of all France's classic wines, consort to Bordeaux's monarch perhaps, but held in special esteem just because of its relative scarcity. (As well as being less reliable from one vintage to the next, the produce of the Burgundy region is a tiny fraction of that of Bordeaux.)

The Pinot grape reaches the apex of its potential on the Côte d'Or, the narrow escarpment running southwest of the city of Dijon, and home to most of Burgundy's famous names. Its narrower northern strip, the Côte de Nuits, which includes such appellations as Gevrey-Chambertin, Nuits-St-Georges and Morey-St-Denis, tends to produce the weightiest style of Burgundian Pinot, with all sorts of meaty notes ranging from the singed skin of roasting poultry to gravy bubbling in the

dish. Further south, the Côte de Beaune, which takes in Aloxe-Corton, Pommard and Volnay among others, specializes in a lighter, gentler Pinot, scented with soft summer fruits and sometimes flowers as well.

The further south of the Côte d'Or you travel, into the Côte Chalonnaise and then the workhorse region of the Mâconnais, the more ordinary the Pinot Noir wines become. At the bottom of the scale, wine labelled Bourgogne Rouge may be a blend of grapes from different sources in the region. It once covered a multitude of sins, but is now increasingly a useful varietal designation for some simple but conscientiously crafted wines.

If the growing season has been relatively chilly or, worse, plagued with intermittent rainfall (as in 2008), the resulting wines can be extremely light, both in colour as well as texture. When a red wine is full of hard acids and bitterly unripe fruit, and feels no richer on the palate than a heavyish rosé, then it's hard to get consumers to see why they should pay the inflated prices.

On the other hand, if burgundy is noted for one thing, it is a resistance to generalizations. Some producers can manage to make densely concentrated wines in even the less auspicious vintages, even while their near neighbours may be wringing their hands. It pays to know who the high fliers are.

Because Pinot often lacks adequate natural sugar to ferment into a full-bodied red that will stay the distance, producers may be permitted to add ordinary cane sugar to the freshly pressed juice. The process is known as chaptalization after its inventor, Jean-Antoine Chaptal. By giving the yeast more sugar to work on, the potential alcohol content of the finished product is raised in the direction of the regional average of 13 per cent. Sometimes, especially when young, it can give off a telltale whiff of burnt sugar, a probable indicator that the winemaker has resorted to fairly heavy chaptalization.

In the best vintages, however, such as 2002, 2005 and 2009, when the Pinot Noir has attained full ripeness, it turns out richly perfumed, exquisitely elegant wines that go at least some way to explaining the heart-stopping prices they sell for. These are the wines that are most worth stashing away for a rainy day.

Autumnal Pinot Noir vines (left) running down towards the town of Aÿ, in Champagne. The inclusion of Pinot in champagne lends it a nuttier, darker hue, and gives the wine depth and good ageing potential.

The beginnings of a red burgundy – Pinot Noir gently fermenting in an open wooden vat (above).

Although it is a red grape, Pinot is hugely important in the making of champagne. The colourless juice is vinified without its skins so that the resulting wine remains white, although if you compare a blended champagne with one that has been made entirely from Chardonnay, you will notice a deeper, nuttier hue in the one that contains Pinot Noir.

Champagne producers consider that Pinot gives their wines depth and the ability to age well. Some champagne, labelled Blanc de Noirs, is made entirely from Pinot Noir and/or the region's other red grape, Pinot Meunier, but is still a white wine. A small amount of still red wine, vaguely Burgundian in style though even more crisply acidic, is made, and may be added to white wine to make rosé champagne. Tiny quantities of pink champagne are made by the painstaking method of infusing the red grape skins briefly in the white juice to tint it to the desired shade.

In the eastern Loire, Pinot Noir is used to make the red (and rosé) versions of Sancerre and Menetou-Salon. These are much lighter in style than burgundy, often with a slightly vegetal hint. They aren't intended for ageing but, served lightly chilled, can make good summer drinking.

Pinot Noir also makes the only red wine of Alsace, again in a typically featherlight and not overly fruity style. Increasingly, though, a handful of producers are starting to take it more seriously, and making wines with the muscle to take some well-judged oak-ageing in their stride.

United States

CALIFORNIA

California has undoubtedly been the most successful region across the board for Pinot Noir outside Burgundy itself. Although they are extremely unlikely to admit it, Burgundy's growers could profitably learn a fair bit from the approach of the more conscientious producers of Pinot Noir in America.

The most successful area to date has been the Carneros AVA, a cool district straddling Napa and Sonoma Counties and benefiting from the coastal fogs that waft in from San Francisco Bay. The afternoons and early evenings in Carneros are sufficiently warm to endow the developing grapes with the exciting flavours of ripe red fruits that are characteristic of the best Pinot wines. At the same time, the cooling influence of those thick mists, which often hang around until mid-morning, ensures adequate levels of fresh acidity, so the wines are impeccably balanced and capable of ageing.

Its ripe fruit intensity means that California Pinot is generally ready for drinking earlier than traditional burgundy, although it does benefit from keeping for a couple of years after release just to allow the nervy edge on those acids to calm down. If the top wines have any noticeable problem, it is that alcohol levels are frequently uncomfortably high. That can result in wines that are very attractive until you swallow them, whereupon they leave a definite smoulder at the back of the throat. There are more balanced wines around now, though, than there were, say, 20 years ago, and the truth is that a lot of them do have the stuffing to carry a weighty alcohol load. Get to know your producers.

In addition to Carneros, parts of Santa Barbara County south of the Bay have proved successful for Pinot Noir, as has the mountainous inland AVA of San Benito, and the AVAs of Russian River Valley and the Santa Cruz Mountains to the north and south of San Francisco respectively.

OREGON

Because of its cooler, damper climate, this Pacific Northwestern state was seen as ideal Pinot territory when the search for appropriate vineyard sites began to gather momentum. Climatically, it is indubitably much closer to Burgundy than most of California, and there are indeed now some stunning wines. The trailblazer was David Lett of Eyrie Vineyards, who first planted Pinot in the 1960s.

It wasn't all plain sailing for many growers. High yields, lack of true physiological ripeness in the grapes and uncertain site selection hampered many early efforts, but Oregon's has been a true tale of dedication to a cause. A succession of good to great vintages since the late 1990s has helped, and some wineries are now showing just what thrilling Pinots the state is capable of making.

Oregon's *premier cru* region is the Willamette Valley AVA, which lies to the west of the Cascade Mountains. A series of smaller AVAs has been demarcated within the overall valley region, with the Dundee Hills and McMinnville looking especially enthralling. The style is generally lighter than in most of California, less meaty but with more accentuated strawberry fruit, and generally approachable sooner.

Terracing a new Pinot Noir vineyard in Oregon (below). The grape of Burgundy is making itself at home in the Pacific Northwest.

Other Regions

NEW ZEALAND

The coolest wine climate in the southern hemisphere has proved perfectly hospitable for Pinot Noir, which is now its most widely planted red grape. Although initial efforts often lacked for enough flesh to cover their bare bones, there are now dozens of world-class producers of top-flight Pinot, and prices have climbed accordingly. The very best display that elusive savoury intensity that adds complexity to the ripe raspberry fruit.

So far, the most exciting wines have come from the Wairarapa region, around the town of Martinborough in the south of the North Island. Most of the cooler South Island is turning out quality Pinot Noir too, from Marlborough and Nelson at the northern end, down through Canterbury and – perhaps most electryfingly of all – Central Otago. If there is a flaw, it is that some wines are made in a more highly extracted, densely coloured, even tannic style than they need to be (some lighter Beaune-like showings would be nice to see), but these are without question among the world's most attractive versions of this most demanding grape.

AUSTRALIA

As with other cool-climate grapes, it is crucial to find the right site for Pinot Noir in Australia, in order to avoid the gloppy or jammy characters

that can so easily spoil it. The Yarra Valley GI in Victoria fits the bill because of its altitude. Western Australia's Margaret River GI has made great strides, while on Tasmania, the cool conditions are responsible for some of the most Burgundian Pinot Noir produced outside France.

SOUTH AFRICA

As in Australia, much of the country is simply too hot to achieve great elegance in wines made from Pinot Noir, and the grape is not that important in South Africa, except for fine sparkling wines. The best varietal red Pinots have so far come from the coastal Walker Bay region.

SOUTH AMERICA

Chile now has some convincing Pinots, grown in the cooler, high-altitude regions such as Casablanca, and even from the hotter environs of the Rapel in Colchagua. The style can be a little overripe and heady, but the fruit is there.

GERMANY

In Germany, they call it Spätburgunder, and it has long been a traditional grape in some of the tiny production of red wines. Typically, they are light as a feather, not much further on from rosé. The southerly region of Baden makes wines with decent fruit, while the northerly Ahr has somehow built a reputation for reds. The odd one, made at the northern limits of world wine-growing, shows true complexity.

A vineyard in the Bannockburn district of Central Otago (above), one of New Zealand's premier regions for growing Pinot Noir.

Hand-plunging the grape skin cap on a tank of Pinot Noir (left) at the Yarra Yering winery in Victoria.

SEMILLON

To many producers, Sémillon suffers a lack of individuality that has destined it to be blended with more fashionable varieties. Yet as the source of rich, golden, honeyed Sauternes, and the unique, aged dry white of Australia, Sémillon is second to none.

WHILE IT IS undoubtedly one of the world's foremost grape varieties, Sémillon has a surprisingly low profile. In the northern hemisphere, it was traditionally not seen very much as an unblended varietal wine. This is largely because, in its native Bordeaux, it is always mixed with Sauvignon Blanc.

However, its highly prized susceptibility in the right conditions to botrytis, the so-called noble rot that concentrates the sugars of overripe grapes by shrivelling them on the vine, makes Sémillon a surefire bet as a dessert-wine producer. The lofty reputation enjoyed by sweet Sauternes and Barsac – in which Sémillon typically represents around four-fifths or more of the blend – has been such that the grape's role in the production of dry white wine has been largely eclipsed.

In Bordeaux today, producers of dry white wine are in the business of pulling out a lot of their Sémillon vines and replacing them with further plantings of its partner Sauvignon. (As we saw when we looked at Sauvignon Blanc, some of the trendiest dry whites of Bordeaux use no Sémillon at all.) That said, it still accounts for far more acreage in the vineyards than Sauvignon, so if it is in decline, the process will be a lengthy one. Many producers frankly consider it to have far less character than its brasher stablemate, being short of aromatic appeal and general *joie-de-vivre*.

To which one can only reply, tell that to the Australians. Semillon (as it is commonly spelt outside France) has been used to produce a varietal dry wine in southern Australia since the 19th century. Its homeland Down Under is the Hunter Valley in New South Wales. True, many growers weren't sure what the variety was, and its traditional (and misleading) name was Hunter Riesling. It does share some of the aromatic characteristics of real Riesling, most notably a minerally aroma of lime-zest, but it almost always gives a fatter, oilier wine than Riesling.

The most peculiar trait a dry Sémillon wine can have is to smell and taste as if it has been wood-matured when it hasn't. Often, there is a distinctly toasty quality to the wine that becomes steadily more pronounced as it ages. Its colour darkens rapidly too, making old Hunter Semillon one of the strangest but most memorable experiences in the world of white wine.

In areas where a lot of cheap bulk wine is produced, Sémillon's easy-going temperament in the vineyard has made it the grape of choice for those who haven't yet caught the Chardonnay bug. Much of South America's vineland, especially in Chile, is carpeted with the variety. An indication of the status in which it is held here is that these are not the wines Chile chooses to boast about on the export markets.

For many, Sémillon provides a relatively trouble-free source of blending material for more fashionable varieties. Although the Bordeaux precedent is to blend it with Sauvignon, Sauvignon is too much in vogue currently to be thought by many producers to need a partner in the bottle. That is why many winemakers, in Australia particularly, have taken to blending Semillon with Chardonnay.

The resulting wines have become bargain-basement alternatives to neat Chardonnay. The lowish prices of these wines indicate how seriously we are being asked to take them. In a hot vintage, where both grapes have yielded similarly rich, fat, silky-textured wines, it is difficult to see what they are supposed to be doing for each other in a blend.

On the other hand, the Sémillon-Sauvignon partnership is nearly always a happy one. The acidity of the latter gives definition to the textural opulence of the former.

The blend makes particular sense in the production of sweet wines. What makes great Sauternes, Barsac and Monbazillac so sought-after, and so extremely long-lived in the bottle, is that a good balance of sugar and acid is present in the wines to start with. Compared to lesser dessert wines from other wine regions, they are hardly ever cloying, despite their massive, syrupy concentration.

Sémillon, a golden-coloured grape with markedly deep green leaves (right) is often used to blend with Sauvignon or Chardonnay. When affected by botrytis (noble rot), it creates the world's finest dessert wines.

FRENCH ORIGINS
Bordeaux.

WHERE ELSE IS IT GROWN?
Australia, South America, a little in South Africa, the USA and New Zealand, and isolated pockets of southern France.

TASTING NOTES
When dry, lime-peel, exotic honey, sometimes has a little of Sauvignon's gooseberry too. Often has a hard mineral purity, even slightly metallic. In the Hunter Valley, deceptive woodiness even when unoaked, turning to burnt toast with age. Blended with Chardonnay, lemon-and-lime squash seems to be the main flavour. When subjected to botrytis for sweet wines, can take on a whole range of exotic fruit characters, but classically has overripe peach or apricot flavour, barley-sugar, honey, allied to a vanilla-custard, *crème brûlée* richness from oak ageing. Australian sweet Semillon can have an emphatically medicinal tinge to it as well.

Bordeaux

Sémillon grapes left on the vine that have been affected by botrytis (right). The shrivelled, blackened grapes will yield a lusciously sweet, concentrated juice.

The elegant Château La Louvière in Pessac-Léognan, Graves (below), owned by the Lurton family. Dry white Bordeaux from the Graves is often the best of its style.

Sémillon's most glorious display in its home region is in the wines of Sauternes and Barsac. At the top of the tree, with a classification all to itself, is the legendary Château d'Yquem, the most expensive sweet wine in the world. The late-summer and autumn climate in Bordeaux provides perfect conditions in many years for the development on Sémillon of the noble rot, botrytis, which causes the berries to moulder and dry out on the vines. As the liquid proportion of the grapes drops, so the sugar in them comes to represent an ever higher percentage, and the result is lusciously sweet, alcoholic, viscous wines of enormous longevity.

If the top wines are so expensive, it is in large part because the more conscientious châteaux take great pains over the harvest. They will hand-select only those berries that are fully rotted, so labour costs are accordingly very high. Most of the wines are aged in at least a proportion of new oak, adding further

dimensions of richness to them. Such wines have long been the inspiration for the production of botrytized Sémillon the world over, and deservedly so.

Elsewhere in Bordeaux, in the making of dry wines, Sémillon rather hangs its head these days. The finger of blame for the notoriously flabby, fruitless dry whites the region once turned out by the vatload came to be pointed its way. But this style has waned as fresh young Sauvignon Blanc, with its tangier fruit, began to show it the door in the late 1980s. As a result, consumers may get the idea that Sémillon is incapable of making great dry wine in Bordeaux, but it ain't necessarily so.

In the northern Graves region of Pessac-Léognan, some of Bordeaux's most illustrious names in dry white wine production still use a greater percentage of Sémillon than Sauvignon in their wines. These include Châteaux Laville-Haut-Brion, Olivier and Latour-Martillac. The results can be breathtaking, the wines having more solidity and savoury concentration than the solo Sauvignon.

Australia

Dry Semillon is one of a handful of unique styles of wine that Australia has contributed to the world. Nor is it a product of some antipodean search for novelty, conceived in a struggle to find ways of doing things that escape the eternal French archetypes. Australia was making Semillons like this in the late 19th century, even though it may have been calling them Hunter Riesling or – even less convincingly – White Burgundy.

The classic Hunter Valley style can be quite austere, as typified by the wines of Tyrrells. Crisp and acerbic in youth, they age to a wonderful roasted-nuts complexity, all achieved without recourse to the expense of oak barrels. Some producers do actually use a modicum of oak to emphasize that natural toastiness. With the tendency now for consumers to drink most wines young, greater stress is being laid on primary fruit flavours – sharp green fruits, usually lime, being the main reference point. Other good Hunter producers are Rothbury, Brokenwood and Lindeman's.

The grape pops up in most Australian regions, though, and fares equally well in areas that are considerably cooler than the Hunter. In the Clare Valley, for instance, Semillon produces a less oily version. As a rough guide, producers who make good Riesling are likely to be reliable for Semillon too: in a cool part of the Clare called Lenswood, Tim Knappstein makes fine, bracingly tart but certainly ageworthy wines.

Western Australia's Margaret River region makes some generously fruity, distinctly smoky Semillons in a style hugely reminiscent of Sauvignon. Evans & Tate is a prime example here.

Although unblended Sauvignon can too often be a disappointment from many parts of Australia, when it is blended with Semillon in the Bordeaux fashion it can produce impressively ripe-fruited wines capable of gaining real complexity with ageing. Cape Mentelle in Margaret River and even St Hallett, in the broiling Barossa Valley region of South Australia, make good blends.

Botrytized, or noble-rotted, Semillon has a long and distinguished tradition here, too. The style may be big and obvious when compared with the top wines of Sauternes, but then there is no particular reason to compare them to Sauternes. De Bortoli in New South Wales was among those who blazed this particular trail, while Peter Lehmann makes a textbook orange-barley-sugar version in the Barossa.

The de Bortoli winery in New South Wales, Australia (below), complete with irrigation canal.

The verdant landscape of South Australia's Clare Valley (below), with Lenswood Vineyard in the foreground. A cool upland district, it can produce bracingly tart but ageworthy Semillons.

SYRAH

Whether recognized as the French grape of the northern Rhône, Syrah, or in its popular guise as Shiraz, in Australia, this grape remains one of the noblest red varieties, fabled for its ability to age majestically for decades.

SUCH IS the success of this grape in Australia that many may know it only by its southern hemisphere name of Shiraz. More of it is grown in Australia than of any other red wine grape, and it appears varietally, as well as in blends with Cabernet Sauvignon and Merlot.

At the pinnacle of its achievements, it shows why it thoroughly deserves its place among the first division of international grape varieties. Australia's most feted red wine, Penfold's Grange, is overwhelmingly composed of Shiraz, usually with only the merest dash of Cabernet as seasoning. In France, it produces some of the most highly prized single-vineyard wines in Europe, wines made in tiny quantities that are sold on allocation to a lucky few favoured customers.

Shiraz produces some of the world's deepest, darkest, most intense red wines, full of black-fruit richness, hot spice and alcoholic power. Then again, it can be used to make the kind of sweetly jammy, oak-smoothed nursery wine that can lure confirmed white wine drinkers on to a bottle of red once in a while.

Syrah, as we should call it when in France, blends well with a number of other grapes, and hangs out with a whole crowd of assorted pals in the wines of the southern Rhône and Languedoc-Roussillon.

The Rhône valley is the ancestral home of Syrah. In viticultural terms, the valley divides into two zones – northern and southern – and represents two very different approaches to the grape. In the south, it makes its way among a large coterie of mostly minor varieties, from the everyday wines of the Côtes du Rhône and Côtes du Ventoux up to the giddy heights of Châteauneuf-du-Pape and its understudy Gigondas. Up to thirteen varieties are permitted in Châteauneuf, of which Syrah generally plays second or third fiddle alongside Mourvèdre, with Grenache playing lead.

It's in the northern Rhône that Syrah really comes into its own. Here, it is the sole red grape, appearing in wines from Hermitage and Côte-Rôtie at the top of the scale to Crozes-Hermitage at the affordable (but still highly reliable) end. The former two can be monumental classic reds that age for at least as long as the very greatest Bordeaux, on account of their precise and complex balance of hugely concentrated fruit, acidity and massive tannic extract. Clenched and surly in youth, they gradually uncoil into the exotically seductive beauties they can be. A topnote of violets frequently adds to the charm.

One of the most commonly encountered descriptions of Rhône Syrah is 'peppery', and even a simple Crozes-Hermitage from a cooperative can display something of that characteristic, although it may vary in intensity from a mild suggestion of spiciness at the back of the throat to the exact and inescapable scent of freshly milled black peppercorns, quite as though the grower had given the wine a few twists of the grinder before sealing the bottle.

Some debate has been occasioned as to whether the famous pepperiness is a varietal property, or whether it isn't at least partly caused by Syrah that hasn't quite attained full ripeness. It is a late-ripening variety, and invariably needs time to show its paces, even in one of the hotter environs of southern France. Compare Australian Shiraz, where the pepperiness is distinctly more muted, if indeed it's really there at all.

In Aussie Shiraz, the fruit is sweetly ripe and right upfront, and the wines rarely have that sharp edge of tannin that northern Rhône examples do. In youth, the softer contours of Shiraz are often derived from the overt influence of creamy oak flavours, so the wine can be drunk sooner. It can be surprisingly delicate aromatically from certain regions, offering a refreshing waft of eucalyptus, rather than the leather and tar and blackberry it traditionally rejoices in. That said, the most concentrated wines are black as sin, and need plenty of time to unwind.

The vibrant blue of the Syrah grape variety (right). Syrah has a unique character most often described as 'peppery', and responds well to oak. In its classic form as the grape of northern Rhône's finest reds, and in Australia as Shiraz, it can make wines that will age for decades.

FRENCH ORIGINS
Northern Rhône.

WHERE ELSE IS IT GROWN?
Australia. Becoming important in the US, South America and South Africa. Traditional in parts of Switzerland.

TASTING NOTES
Can smell of almost any dark purple fruit – blackberries, blackcurrants, black cherries, damsons, plums. Freshly ground black pepper in the northern Rhône. Exotic flavours can include liquorice, ginger, dark chocolate, often a distinct floral note, too, like violets. Cool topnote of mint characteristic in parts of South Australia. Aged wines can take on something of the gaminess of old Pinot Noir.

Given that there is so much Shiraz in Australia, it isn't surprising that a lot of it finds its way into very basic wines. A cloyingly sweet, jammy, offputting style is depressingly widespread. On the other hand, its use in thoroughly innovative red sparkling wines in both sweetish and powerfully dry, tannic styles, has been a head-turner. Relinquish any memories of wafer-thin fizzy red Lambrusco. Sparkling Shiraz is a muscled-up blockbuster. I tend to prefer those wines with a little residual sugar, rather than heavy tannic fizz.

France

The greatest producers in Rhône Syrah are now ranked up with Bordeaux's and Burgundy's finest. This is still, however, a fairly recent phenomenon. While the burly red wines of Hermitage had always had a lofty reputation among British wine enthusiasts, the production of the region as a whole was not held in particularly high regard. When the influential American wine critic Robert Parker began, in the 1980s, to rate some of the best wines of Marcel Guigal (now one of the northern Rhône's superstars) as the equals of the great vintages of Mouton-Rothschild, the international wine trade was persuaded to take notice.

That development inevitably prompted the producers to put up their prices, but it has to be said that the best had certainly been undervalued in the past. These are wines with the same sort of structure and ageing capacity as Cabernet-based clarets (often even more muscularly built, in fact) and their flavours resemble no other red wines in France.

Of the northern Rhône appellations for varietal Syrah, Hermitage is traditionally the biggest and beefiest. Although solidly constructed, the wines are not without grace and elegance, and the fruit flavour can be surprisingly lighter than the reputation – more raspberries than blackberries. At their most immense, though, these are densely textured, ferociously dark stunners, but retaining their primary fruit well into their maturity.

Côte-Rôtie is the appellation that has created all the excitement in recent years, the most frenetic buzz being around Guigal's three single-vineyard wines – La Mouline, La Landonne and La Turque. These are mind-blowingly concentrated expressions of fine Syrah that sell for sky-high prices. Up to 20 per cent of the white grape, Viognier, is permitted in Côte-Rôtie under the appellation regulations, and can add a bewitching note of apricot to Syrah's blackberry.

St-Joseph makes slightly lighter wines, piercingly blackcurrant in the good years, while the bottom-line appellation of Crozes-Hermitage is well worth trying as an introduction to the flavours of Rhône Syrah. I say 'bottom-line', but there are growers now making Crozes as opaque and intense and long-lived as some Hermitage.

The final appellation of the northern Rhône, Cornas, is an odd one, in that its Syrah is the least immediately recognizable. The wines are often rather tough, and lacking the benefit of youthful fruit, or they can simply taste like blended wines from appellations further south such as Châteauneuf-du-Pape. Some growers are working with the grain of Cornas Syrah to make some excitingly individual, if austere, wines. Long bottle-ageing is mandatory.

In the southern Rhône, and down into the Languedoc, Syrah is blended with many other red grapes, among them Grenache, Mourvèdre, Cinsault and Carignan. Unless a producer has used a particularly high percentage of Syrah, the grape may not be individually perceptible in these wines, though it does beef up the structure.

The chapel and vines on the famous hill of Hermitage (below), overlooking the river Rhône and the towns of Tournon and Tain l'Hermitage.

Australia

Shiraz has been the pre-eminent red grape variety in Australia for as long as anyone can remember, but it is only since the 1970s that there has been a significant impetus towards producing world-class wine from it. At its most humdrum, Shiraz is a rather gloopy plum-jam sort of wine with too much heavy oak influence in it, so that the toffeeish sweetness of its aftertaste can be quite sickly. Thankfully, there are more than enough accomplished Shiraz producers to make for a brighter picture overall.

It's all a question, as so often, of microclimate. In the hotter GIs, such as the Hunter and Barossa Valleys, Shiraz is responsible for the thickest, most opulently fruity of all Australia's reds. In the warmer central sector of Victoria, the Goulburn Valley GI is home to some especially concentrated Shirazes of great aromatic intensity.

The red soil of Coonawarra is as distinguished a hotbed of Shiraz as it is of Cabernet Sauvignon, producing subtly spiced wines, as well as accessibly fruit-filled offerings, not all of which use oak.

From old vines in parts of the Barossa Valley, Shiraz results in small amounts of extraordinarily deep, resonant and complex wines that can stand next to top Côte-Rôtie.

The Hill of Grace vineyard, owned by Henschke (above), in the Barossa Valley, South Australia. The Shiraz vines planted here are over 100 years old.

Other Regions

SOUTH AFRICA

As in Australia, it took a while for Shiraz to persuade its growers that it was worth taking seriously as a variety. Inspired by success elsewhere, some impressive Shiraz is now emerging. It should work after all, given the sultry climatic conditions the grape loves. Stellenbosch and Paarl are among the premier growing regions.

CALIFORNIA

Despite the West Coast fashion for Rhône grape varieties, Syrah (as it tends to be known here) has been slow to establish itself as an important grape. The trend so far has been to make wines with French levels of acidity and memorably aromatic fruit, but not quite the degree of concentration of the most well-bred Côte-Rôtie. San Luis Obispo has the most extensive plantings, but Santa Barbara and Napa may well be the best regions for it.

CHILE

Chile started to flex its muscles with Syrah only in the 1990s, with results that are already beginning to intrigue. Rhône comparisons are plentiful, with wines from various sub-zones of Colchagua, together with San Antonio and coastal Casablanca, beginning to look very tasty. The best will age well.

Orderly rows of Shiraz vines at Franschhoek's Bellingham Vineyards, Paarl, South Africa (above).

Vineyards of Joseph Phelps, (left), a trend-setter for quality Syrah in California, in springtime Napa Valley.

RIESLING

Germany's noble white grape variety, Riesling, is a versatile performer. It is prized in northern Europe and the southern hemisphere for its ability to produce classic sweet whites as well as impeccable dry wines.

The Riesling (right) is a hardy, frost-resistant vine, which makes it ideal for the cool vineyards of northern Europe. Riesling can produce long-lived wines of intense aroma and character, ranging in style from bone-dry to lusciously sweet.

THE ONLY FINE wine grape of international importance not to have originated in France, Riesling is the great speciality of German winemaking. Its only base in France is in the Alsace region, a sheltered northeastern enclave between the Vosges mountains and the Rhine valley that has intermittently, usually by force, been a geopolitical part of Germany. Like Sémillon, Riesling is capable of making impeccably dry wines of surprising longevity, as well as lusciously sweet dessert wines affected by the noble rot, botrytis, but unlike Sémillon it also runs the whole gamut of styles in between.

In recent years, Riesling has come to be considered the most underrated of all the top grapes. Why this should be so when it is such a versatile performer might seem a mystery, but is at least partly explicable by the wholly irrational association in many consumers' minds of Riesling with cheap, extraneously sweetened German wine such as Liebfraumilch – the low-alcohol, low-acid introduction to the world of wine that drinkers of my own generation cut our teeth on.

Although Liebfraumilch may not have quite the same purchase on the tastes of young consumers that it once had, it remains infuriatingly confusable with quality German wine. The bottles look the same as top-quality Rhine Rieslings and, even though it's always worth looking for the name of this grape on a German wine label, the good wines turn out to share the same basic characteristics – lightness and often a delicate sweetness (albeit from natural grape sugars) – as the slosh.

How to persuade people that these are in fact much better wines? Only time and tasting practice will tell. For one thing, the clear varietal characters of the grape can be breathtakingly beautiful, a whoosh of citric freshness like squeezing a lime, together with mineral notes and often something like the

flesh of a juicy-ripe peach, all suspended in a wine that then belies its apparent fragility by surviving intact in the bottle over many years. There is far more joy in a ten-year-old Riesling of perhaps 7 per cent alcohol than there is in a ten-year-old, 13 per cent Sauvignon.

Because Germany's vineyards are at the northern extremity of where vines can be grown, the country's quality classification system developed along the lines of assessing just how ripe the grapes were when harvested, and therefore how potentially sweet the resulting wines would be. Severely low winter-time temperatures might then arrest the fermentation of the wines, leaving them low in alcohol and retaining a degree of unfermented grape sugar. These were precisely the attributes that aficionados came to treasure in them.

International tastes in wine provoked an experimental movement in Germany in the 1980s and 90s to ferment some of the wines – Rieslings and others – to dryness. Initially, many of these wines were disastrously unbalanced, and the technique appeared to work better with other varieties than Riesling, but more rounded wines have since emerged.

Riesling always gives a high-acid wine, which is perhaps best offset in Germany by some level of natural sweetness, so that even those at the drier end of the spectrum (the styles known as Kabinett and Spätlese) have a softening edge on them. In warmer climes, there is generally enough ripeness and alcohol to balance the high acidity, making for appetizing dry wines that can age well.

This has traditionally been the case in Alsace and the cooler parts of Australia, the world's two best sources of dry Riesling. Other countries have appeared to struggle with the grape. In time, cool-climate New Zealand will doubtless become a reliable producer of outstanding dry Rieslings, but for the time being, there are too many unfocused wines that taste vaguely of boiled sweets. It will not go down well in the Rhine and Mosel valleys to say so, but it may well be that the more success producers outside Europe have with Riesling,

ORIGINS
Germany.

WHERE ELSE IS IT GROWN?
Alsace. Australia and New Zealand. Austria and northern Italy. Some in the United States and Canada.

TASTING NOTES
Nearly always has the scent of lime, whether bitter zests or freshly pressed juice. Riper German ones can have softer fruit like ripe peach or apricot, as well as a gentle floral aroma. In Alsace, there is a very austere mineral quality in the wines and a texture on the palate like sharpened steel. A whiff of petrol (or gasoline) flowing from the pump generally comes with age, although some Australian wines can display it quite young.

the greater the chance that people may come back to an enjoyment of German wines, freed of the inaccurate preconceptions that still stand in their way.

At the sweetest and richest end of the spectrum, Riesling makes some of the most enticing, and beautifully balanced, botrytized wines in the world. The Beerenauslese and Trockenbeerenauslese offerings of Germany and Austria, as well as the most carefully tended Noble Rieslings of Australia, South Africa and the United States, all combine fresh acidity with layers of honey-soaked, citrus-spiked lusciousness.

Germany

Riesling is grown in nearly all of the wine regions of Germany, and has since the 1990s been the country's most widely planted variety. It is in many ways particularly well suited to the cold climates it encounters there, because the tough stems of its vines enable them to cope with the worst the winters can throw at them.

The drawback comes at the other end of the annual cycle, when ripening the grapes is something of a gamble against the elements. Picked too early, Riesling can be full of hard, unripe acidity. Waiting for the right levels of ripeness can often mean leaving the bunches hanging into November, when French growers have long since picked, pressed and fermented, and when the weather is so bitter that it can be hard to get a natural fermentation going.

With all that in mind, much effort and funding has gone into crossing Riesling with other German varieties, and even crossing the crosses with Riesling and others. The aim has been to try to perfect a grape that will give the fresh fruit flavours of Riesling, as well as its invaluable susceptibility to botrytis, but with a more reliable ripening pattern. A handful of these have yielded goodish results, but few seriously believe they can take the place of Riesling as Germany's premier performer.

The top classification for German wines, their equivalent of the French *appellation contrôlée*, is *Prädikatswein* (literally, wine with distinction). Within this class, there are five types of wine, measured according to the amount of natural sweetness in them. In ascending order, they are: Kabinett, Spätlese, Auslese, Beerenauslese and Trockenbeerenauslese. The suffix '-lese' means 'picked', and the time of picking is specifically indicated in the prefix, from Spätlese (late-picked, i.e. just after the normal harvesting time) to Trockenbeerenauslese or TBA (meaning berries picked outside – that is, after – the main harvest, which are dried and shrivelled with sugar-concentrating noble rot).

The famous steep vineyards of the Mosel region (below) where the Riesling vines tumble down towards the Mosel river. Such steep sites means hand-picking is the only option at harvest-time.

Any of the first three styles may be fermented out to total dryness to become Trocken (dry) wines, or halfway in the case of wines labelled Feinherb. Some super-sweet berries are left on the vines until nearer Christmas, in some vintages even into the new year, and are picked at the crack of dawn when they are half-frozen. During the pressing, some of the crystals of ice that represent the water content of the grapes are removed and the very sweet juice that hasn't frozen is then fermented. This style is known, for obvious reasons, as Eiswein (ice wine).

The fullest, most concentrated Rieslings have traditionally come from the Rheingau, where the vineyard has long been dominated by Riesling plantings. Here, the best producers make wines that are as expressive of their particular vineyard locations as any illustrious Burgundy *grand cru*.

A non-Trocken Riesling from the Rheingau is generally around 10 per cent alcohol, relatively heady in German terms, and there is a rounded, often honeyed feel to the best of them. Legend insists that the Rheingau was the region where the first noble-rotted wines

were accidentally produced, many years before the technique became known in Sauternes.

To the west of the Rheingau, the Nahe also has a preponderance of Riesling, although here it is a more recent development as a result of the region's standing having risen considerably in the last few years. There are some very promising young growers here now.

The other two neighbouring Rhine regions are Rheinhessen and Pfalz (the latter originally known in English as the Palatinate). Riesling has made great strides in the Pfalz, where an almost tropical aromatic intensity is the house style of the most talented producers, although the wines are still possessed of that traditionally delicate structure and finesse.

To the northwest, and centred on the city of Trier, the Mosel-Saar-Ruwer region produces the lightest, most exquisitely subtle and refined versions of Riesling made anywhere in the world. Alcohol levels may be as low as 7 per cent, and the aromatic profile of the wines so astonishingly rarefied that a sniff at the glass can be like breathing in pure mountain air. The vineyards are planted on vertiginously steep slopes on either side of the river, so any thought of harvesting with motor vehicles is out of the question. Enforced rigorous hand-picking of carefully selected grapes should go some way to explaining the prices.

Vineyards looking down to the village of Ungstein, in the Pfalz region of Germany (above). The traditional style of Riesling wines here is both aromatic and tremendously delicate.

Schloss Johannisberg, looking down over its Riesling vineyards (left), in the Rheingau. Rheingau Rieslings are traditionally the fullest, most concentrated in style.

Alsace

The 15th-century church in the midst of vineyards at Hunawihr, Alsace (above).

Anybody familiar with the wines of Alsace may tend more readily to associate them with the highly perfumed, positively decadent flavours of Gewurztraminer and Pinot Gris than with the steely austerity of Riesling. It is, however, an open secret in the region that Riesling is considered the noblest of them all, partly because the acidity levels it usually attains mean that the resulting wines have a good long life ahead of them. The variety has been here since the 15th century, and today comprises over 20 per cent (and counting) of the vineyard land. Everybody loves Riesling.

It is in the hilly Haut-Rhin district of Alsace that most of the Riesling is concentrated. The best plots are those that are protected from the wind so that the ripening of the grapes is not inhibited, although the climate of this sheltered region is generally much more benign than what German growers have to contend with. Unusually for a fine wine grape, the amount of fruit the vines are permitted to yield under the appellation regulations is quite high, without the wines themselves necessarily lacking anything in full-blown aromatic intensity.

Most Alsace Riesling is made in an assertively bone-dry style, with around 12 per cent alcohol and rapier-like acidity. They are the only Alsace wines that are not especially enjoyable if drunk young, most requiring at least five years to begin to settle down. In their youth, they have a highly strung, quite taut feel on the palate, leavened with some bracing citric fruit, comparable to freshly squeezed lime juice.

In addition to the basic dry wines, there are two designations for sweeter styles. The lighter of the two is Vendange Tardive (meaning late harvest); in a warm late summer the grapes are left on the vines to achieve higher sugar levels that convert to a delicately sweet wine. In the right conditions, ie. damp misty mornings giving way to mild sunny daytime weather, Riesling will botrytize, just as it does in Germany. The hugely concentrated syrupy wines that result are called Sélection de Grains Nobles – among the most appealingly balanced noble-rotted dessert wines in all of France.

Certain of the best vineyard sites in Alsace have been designated *grands crus* since the mid-1980s. These wines should have a noticeable extra dimension of intensity in the flavour, and are inevitably sold for higher prices. Prominent among the best of the *grand cru* sites for Riesling are Hengst, Rangen, Schoenenberg and Sommerberg. Lower yields contribute to their unearthly concentration.

Steeply shelving vineyards form the backdrop to the typically alsacien *architecture of Trimbach's premises at Ribeauvillé, Alsace (right).*

Other Regions

AUSTRALIA

There was once more Riesling in Australia than there was Chardonnay, which may come as a surprise to those who primarily associate Australian white wine with the sun-drenched oaky flavours of the latter grape. Because it needs a certain amount of acidity to give it sharp definition, Riesling is much more successful in the cooler areas of the country, such as the Clare Valley in South Australia and parts of Western Australia such as Mount Barker.

The Australian style is richer and fatter than the European models. In youth, they have pungent lemon-and-lime fruit and oily texture. Sometimes, most notably in wines from Clare Valley, they also display those heady petrol fumes that German and Alsace Rieslings only tend to take on with bottle-age. Despite their smoother angles, the most sensitively made Australian Rieslings still show good acid balance to maintain that sense of freshness without which Riesling wines are lost.

Many growers are more conscientious about their Riesling than they are about any other variety, ensuring its careful handling every step of the way from harvesting to its treatment in the winery, an approach that is paying off handsomely in the depth and ageing potential the wines now boast.

As well as the dry styles, there are also some extremely fine botrytized Rieslings being made in Australia. Indeed, for many people (myself included), these just have the edge, for

thorough-going complexity and balance, over the country's nobly rotted Semillons. Attaining immense levels of concentration, the wines retain their citric freshness, with a flavour profile like lemon marmalade.

NEW ZEALAND

New Zealand's cooler climes should be ideally suited to the production of good dry Riesling. In fact, there was a tendency until fairly recently to make an indeterminate medium-dry sort of wine, with a twangy, not-quite-wholesome fruit quality not a million miles from boiled sweets. The South Island has lately led the way in producing some fresh, clean, impeccably limey Rieslings of great promise. When vintage conditions permit, many producers also make a botrytized Riesling.

NORTH AMERICA

Cooler parts of California and, particularly, Washington State have seen tentative plantings of Riesling, but it's fair to say the grape has not proved the hottest property commercially in the US. Late-picked Washington versions can be sublime, though. Further north, in Canada, Riesling is turning out some convincing wines in the province of Ontario. Some of Canada's fabled Icewines use Riesling; the best can challenge the pick of German Eiswein.

Harvesting Riesling grapes in the depths of winter (above) in Ontario, Canada. The frozen grapes are destined for Canada's fabled Icewine.

Checking the progress of bunches of ripening Riesling (left), in South Australia's Clare Valley, one of the grape's best growing areas.

MERLOT

Historically used in the blended reds of Bordeaux, Merlot's fame is founded on its partnership with Cabernet Sauvignon. Its reputation as a solo performer has been earned more recently.

FOR WINEMAKERS all over the world, Merlot is the significant other of Cabernet Sauvignon, its truest blending friend and stalwart partner. But whereas Cabernet came to be seen internationally as capable of performing in its own right, Merlot was not generally thought to have the wherewithal to fly solo – at least not at first.

Merlot may have been used unblended for industrial quantities of everyday quaffing wine in northern Italy, but in its homeland of Bordeaux, where it originated, the red wines are always blends. Moreover, the first-growth wines of the Haut-Médoc and Graves are all based on a grape mix in which Cabernet Sauvignon predominates.

And yet, there is far more of Merlot planted in Bordeaux than there is of Cabernet. (It is in fact now the most widely planted grape in France.) While it may be a junior partner on the left bank of the Gironde, though, look to the right bank, and we find the origins of its international reach. In the two best areas here, Pomerol and St-Emilion, Merlot has the starring role.

Some Pomerol properties use virtually all Merlot in their reds; the leader of the pack, Château Pétrus, is nearly all Merlot down to the last five per cent or so of Cabernet Franc. You only have to consider the stratospheric prices commanded by Pétrus to realize that Merlot has no need to hide its light under a bushel of Cabernet Sauvignon. The overall percentage of Merlot in the wines of St-Emilion is a little lower, with proportionately more Cabernet Franc, but it is still the capstone variety, prized for its gentler style.

As in all regions where blended wines are the historical norm, producers will mix and match the proportions of Cabernet and Merlot, depending on vintage conditions. Merlot has the advantage of ripening earlier than Cabernet Sauvignon, meaning that late rain or a sudden cool snap at the end of the growing season, arriving just in time to spoil the chances of great Cabernet, can be at least partially offset by blending in more of the already-harvested Merlot. Even in the better years (such as 1990), Merlot can often out-perform Cabernet in producing a healthy ripe crop.

Stylistically, what Merlot does for Cabernet in the wines of the Médoc is smooth away some of their harder edges. A claret containing, say,

The plump, blue Merlot (right), an early-ripening grape, produces soft, rich wines – often described as 'fleshy' – that harmonize well with the more structured Cabernet Sauvignon.

35 per cent Merlot will have a softer mouth-feel than one where it is limited to a mere 10 per cent. There is an undoubtedly slightly sweeter edge to it than the surlier Cabernet displays.

Outside Bordeaux, Merlot really started to branch out on its own in the California of the 1980s. Varietal Merlot had been produced there prior to this, but the tendency was, as with the Cabernets, to over-extract its tannins. In the latter part of the 80s, softer, gentler Merlots for everyday drinking began to be made. Its role as a red-wine-without-tears saw plantings increase fivefold in the decade from the mid-80s to the mid-90s as Merlot-mania took hold. Washington State also turns out plenty of uncomplicated, velvet-soft Merlot. The result

of that is that knowledgeable wine enthusiasts have stopped treating Merlot as a serious wine. A rethink among producers is now due.

In the southern hemisphere, it has been a conspicuous success in Chile, where the most ambitious Merlots in districts like Rapel are now beginning to rival Pomerol for sumptuous depth of impact. Argentina's plantings are gaining ground too. Outstanding Merlots are cropping up in South Africa, where a spicy, even gamey complexity distinguishes the best.

In Australia, solo Merlot has only lately begun to find its feet. The grape is still more usually seen as a blending partner for Cabernet after the Bordeaux model, an approach common in New Zealand too.

FRENCH ORIGINS
Bordeaux, especially the Libournais on the right bank of the Gironde, which includes St-Emilion and Pomerol.

WHERE ELSE IS IT GROWN?
Throughout central and eastern Europe, from Switzerland to Bulgaria. United States. Argentina. Some in Chile, Australia, New Zealand, South Africa.

TASTING NOTES
At its ripest, soft purple fruits such as blackberries and black plums. In cooler climates, it can have a distinct vegetal streak in it, like French (green) beans or asparagus. If the sun gets to it, there may be a suggestion of dried fruit such as raisins or even fruitcake. Rounded out with oak in the best wines of Pomerol and California, it can also take on a textural richness that has overtones of melted chocolate or possibly Turkish Delight.

France

The fairy-tale Château Ausone (above), in St-Emilion, set amid its vines.

The legendary Château Pétrus, Pomerol (below). Oil burners are still used in the vineyards as late as May to protect the early-ripening Merlot from frost damage.

Merlot's French fiefdom is on the right bank in Bordeaux. There, it dominates the communes of Pomerol and St-Emilion. While red wines from the latter district are characteristically composed of around two-thirds Merlot with perhaps just a splash of Cabernet Sauvignon, in Pomerol the proportion may be more like nine-tenths Merlot, with no Cabernet Sauvignon at all.

Differences in character between the wines of the two communes can be quite marked, with the top wines of Pomerol having a seriousness and austerity about them, together with something of the savoury, herbal overtones found in left-bank Cabernet. St-Emilion wines, on the other hand, for all that there may be less Merlot in them, are often softer and more approachable earlier on. Despite the popular assumption that Merlot-based wines mature more quickly than those dominated by Cabernet Sauvignon, St-Emilions and Pomerols can be quite as long-lived as the finest offerings of the Médoc, as witness Château Pétrus.

In 1955, on the centenary of the original Bordeaux classification, St-Emilion endowed itself with a similar league-table of properties. In contrast to the entrenched near-immutability of the left bank, however, the proprietors of St-Emilion undertook to update their classification every ten years. There may be little change from decade to decade, but that is precisely because they know their wines will be rigorously reassessed, and so the motivation to maintain standards is compelling. Top spot is shared by two châteaux: Cheval Blanc and Ausone.

Alone among the premier communes of Bordeaux, Pomerol has never been subjected to the trials of classification, and there are no plans for one. The legendary Pétrus would no doubt occupy pole position in any such notional system, followed by the likes of Châteaux Clinet, l'Evangile, Le Pin, Lafleur, Vieux-Château-Certan and Trotanoy.

Less illustrious Merlot-based wines come from what are known as the satellite areas of St-Emilion, a group of small communes that form a northeasterly fringe to St-Emilion itself, and are all allowed to append its name to their own – Montagne, Lussac, Puisseguin and St-Georges. In good vintages, when the grander properties can fetch dizzyingly high prices for their wines, some of the satellite wines can represent exemplary value. The most aromatically attractive, for my money, tend to come from Puisseguin and Lussac.

Elsewhere, Merlot has made great inroads among the varietal wines being produced in the Languedoc under the catchall Vin de Pays d'Oc designation, and it also has a part to play in some of the traditional appellations of the southwest. In Cahors, for example, it performs its time-honoured diplomatic role, tempering the sternness of the Auxerrois and Tannat grapes.

Rest of the World

UNITED STATES

Merlot is the red wine of choice for those California and Washington wine-drinkers who want the richness and structure of a good red, without having to age it until it's soft enough to drink. In that respect, it's very much Cabernet for beginners. The benchmark style is now ripe red fruit with a lick of sweet oak and gentle tannins. Cooler areas of the eastern States, such as the Long Island AVA, are now producing some more complex wines with something of the structure of Bordeaux.

ITALY

It's fair to say that Merlot doesn't enjoy a particularly exalted reputation in Italy, although large swathes of its wine industry – especially in the northeastern areas of the Veneto, Friuli and Piave – would be lost without it. The tendency is to make a juicy, but light-toned wine, perfectly suited to lunchtime quaffing by the carafe. In hotter years, however, and from producers prepared to limit their yields, there can be a little meaty complexity to the wines.

In the hotbed of viticultural dynamism that is Tuscany, one or two of the smart operators are achieving fine results with Merlot. Producers such as Lodovico Antinori, with his varietal Merlot, Masseto, are showing that the variety can make full-blooded, ageworthy wines that are the equals of the monumental Cabernet and Sangiovese super-Tuscans.

CHILE

Merlot is now responsible for most of the greatest red wines of Chile. It was for a long time mistaken in the vineyards for another grape, Carmenère (also found in Bordeaux), and wines labelled Merlot often have a percentage of Carmenère in them. The fruit expression in these wines is little short of stunning. They age well, but are also drinkable at barely more than a year old. Merlots from Rapel have just about the best price-quality ratio of any red wines in the southern hemisphere.

OTHER SOUTHERN HEMISPHERE

The Australasian countries were late starters in the varietal Merlot stakes, the custom having been to blend it traditionally with Cabernet Sauvignon. Hawkes Bay, New Zealand, is

Merlot is the most widely planted red grape variety in Romania (left), making soft, easy-drinking reds.

responsible for some sharply defined, plummy Merlot now. The Barossa Valley and McLaren Vale are good Australian sources.

In South Africa, especially Stellenbosch, the grape has emerged from its eternal partnership with Cabernet to make some outstandingly complex, full-fleshed wines unblended.

OTHER EUROPE

Merlot has traditionally been a source of soft, everyday reds throughout eastern Europe (especially Bulgaria and Romania), and it enjoys particular favour in parts of Switzerland, producing mostly light, easy-drinking wines in the Italian-speaking southern canton of Ticino.

Barrel cellars at Lodovico Antinori (below), Tuscany. Antinori is one of the band of top Tuscan producers creating stunning varietal Merlots.

CHENIN BLANC

Chenin Blanc's wide stylistic repertoire has made it the focal grape variety in the central vineyards of the Loire valley. Put through its paces in Vouvray, it runs the gamut of dry to sweet, and sparkling, wines.

PERHAPS THE most misunderstood of all the noble grape varieties, Chenin Blanc is the backbone of white winemaking in the Loire valley. While it undoubtedly has a very distinct and recognizable profile in the wines it can produce, it has experienced difficulties in making friends among consumers for two reasons.

One is that, like Riesling, it has a wide stylistic repertoire, ranging all the way from the uncompromisingly bone-dry to luxurious botrytized dessert wines with decades of ageing potential. Nothing wrong with that, except that, in the past, the labelling on Chenin wines from the Loire has been low on information about the style of the wine.

The other hurdle for newcomers to clear is that the drier wines are not over-endowed with the sort of immediately obvious commercial appeal found in young Sauvignon Blanc. Put crudely, they are quite often not very nice. There is an aromatic character to them, but it is composed of rather weird elements – a mixture of brushed steel, old honey and damp. The classic tasting description often heard is 'wet wool'. Add to that the fact that Chenin is nearly always loaded with teeth-grinding acidity, and it is easier to understand why this is not a grape likely to be top of anyone's list of all-time favourites.

Learning to appreciate Chenin requires a more precise knowledge of when to drink the different styles of wines than is the case with most other white wine varieties.

In the Loire, Vouvray is the most important appellation for Chenin. Its wines span the spectrum from dry to sweet, as well as sparkling wine made by the champagne method. The dry wines, increasingly labelled as such (*sec*) these days, can be delicious immediately on release, when they can display exhilarating fruit flavours, and that boldly assertive acid acts as a seasoning in the way that lemon juice does in a fruit coulis. After a year, they seem to lose that fruit and slump into a prolonged sulk;

tasted again at five or six years old, they have developed a honeyed softness that throws that dryness into relief.

In a hotter vintage, the winemaker may choose to leave some of the ripe natural sugars of the grape in the finished wine. This off-dry or medium-dry style is known as *demi-sec*. It can be the most supremely refreshing example of its kind to be found anywhere in France. The delicate note of lingering sweetness tenderizes the prickly acids in a hugely appetizing way.

If the grapes reach a level of sticky-sweet overripeness that the French call *surmaturité*, then the resulting wine is known as *moelleux*. These are not quite the richest dessert wines – they still have that spiky streak of acidity running through them – but they do have a lush coating of honey and caramel.

In years when botrytis has freely developed, some producers may make a fully botrytized wine. This will often be entitled *Sélection*, because it involves selecting only the most extensively shrivelled berries from the vine, for maximum impact. Even then, the layers of concentrated sweetness have a discernible tartness at the centre, so that the overall effect is more toffee-apple than crème brûlée.

Elsewhere in the world, Chenin's malleability has made it something of a workhorse grape. That is certainly the case in the hotter regions of the United States and Australia, where its most widespread use has been as blending fodder, to add a tingle of acid and prevent basic white wines from tasting flabby. It is very extensively planted in South Africa, where it often goes under the alias of Steen. While a lot of it inevitably disappears into the blending vats, some at least is turned into fresh, fruit-filled, even complex whites of almost miraculous crispness, given the climate.

Grapes with naturally high acidity are often a good bet for the production of champagne-method sparkling wine, where a thin, relatively neutral base wine gives the best results. In the Loire, as well as sparkling Vouvray, Saumur is a good source of such fizz, as is the wider regional appellation of Crémant de Loire.

Chenin Blanc (right) is a high-acid grape that favours the cooler climates of the Loire valley. Here, its acidity and susceptibility to botrytis are its keys to success, making fine sparkling wine and exquisite sweet wines that retain a thread of refreshing sharpness.

FRENCH ORIGINS
The central Loire valley –
Anjou-Saumur and Touraine.

WHERE ELSE IS IT GROWN?
South Africa. Also California,
Australia, New Zealand, and
a little in Argentina.

TASTING NOTES
When young and dry, tart green
apple and pear, occasionally
something a little more exotic
(passion fruit) in a good year.
Mineral, even metallic, hardness
on the palate, though often with
paradoxical underlying hint of
honey. Can have a dry nuttiness
(walnuts) and an indeterminately
damp smell, like old newspaper
or wet woollens. Sweeter
styles get progressively more
honeyed without losing the
tingly, appley acidity woven
through them.

Loire

Despite its appearance in many areas outside Europe, no region makes more of Chenin Blanc than does the Loire. It is the most important white grape variety in the two central parts of the valley – Anjou-Saumur to the west, and Touraine in the east.

In Anjou, particularly, cultivating Chenin is something of a challenge. So far north, the grape is a notoriously slow ripener and, as summers in these parts are not exactly torrid, a lot of Anjou Chenin is very acerbic and raw-tasting – not a style that would find many imitators beyond France's borders. Then again, that is exactly how the locals like it to taste.

Autumns, though, are damp and warm enough to permit the regular development of the noble rot, botrytis. It is in Anjou that the premier appellations for botrytized Chenin are found: Coteaux du Layon, which encircles the tiny and very fine enclave of Bonnezeaux (an AOC in its own right), and Quarts de Chaume. In the best years, these wines are fully the equal of great

An unusually fine summer's day blazes down on the Chenin vines in the tiny AC of Bonnezeaux in Anjou (below), where some of the Loire's finest botrytized Chenins are produced.

Sauternes and Barsac, because they have that nerve-centre of acidity that keeps them going into a well-balanced old age.

The lesser-known appellation of Coteaux de l'Aubance makes some reasonably good, though much less rich, sweet wines, from grapes that shrivel on the vines but are only rarely tinged with botrytis. Drink them young.

In the west of Anjou is Savennières, the appellation that many consider to be the highest expression of dry Chenin anywhere in the wine world. In their first flush, these intellectually demanding wines make no concessions to drinkability, tasting hard as nails and tightly clenched. Over maybe seven or eight years, they open out into an austere but profoundly beautiful maturity, full of minerals, bitter apples and bracing Atlantic fresh air. The word 'racy', when applied to wine, might have been coined just for Savennières. Within the appellation is a single-ownership AOC called Coulée-de-Serrant, run along biodynamic principles (see entry, Loire section).

Travelling eastwards into Saumur, we enter fizz territory. Sparkling Saumur is made by fermenting the wine a second time in the bottle to produce carbon dioxide, exactly as for champagne. Made only, or almost entirely, from Chenin, it usually has quite a snap to it, and is dead dry. Served well-chilled on a hot day, it makes an appealing aperitif quaff.

In Touraine, the most important appellation of all for Chenin Blanc is Vouvray. Together with its lesser-known and less distinguished neighbour to the south, Montlouis, Vouvray puts the Chenin through its paces, making it dry, *demi-sec*, *moelleux*, botrytized or fizzy, according to taste. Quality is highly variable, and the wines – as elsewhere – are very vintage-dependent, but when it shines, it really shines.

The wines of the best growers in Vouvray constitute an invaluable introduction to this underestimated grape, with which it is worth persevering. You'll find the odd one that has the mildly vomity smell of dried Parmesan, while others are reminiscent of stale nuts. Then suddenly, there'll be one full of green apple tartness, maybe the sharpness of passion-fruit, with honey lurking underneath, finishing with the taste of freshly shelled walnuts, and you've arrived in Chenin country.

Other Regions

SOUTH AFRICA

Chenin, or Steen as it is very often termed, is put to practically the same sort of versatile use in South Africa as it is in the Loire. It's even used in some of the monumental fortified wines for which the Cape was once famous. Although plantings have fallen off in recent years, this is still the country's most widely grown grape.

At one time, the drier styles didn't tend to be that remarkable, being rather neutral, uninspiring house-white stuff. These days, though, that's all changing. Dry Cape Chenin can now fill the mouth with a gum-cleansing feel like biting into a just-picked apple. They have body and definite varietal identity, and they are full of the sharp aromatic definition more logically to be expected from the cool northerly climate of the Loire. Some producers subject their wines to a modicum of oak, which they seem to take in their stride.

Fantastic wines are made from noble-rotted Chenin, when the flavours of tropical fruit, honey, bitter orange peel and barley-sugar all seem to mingle in what are some of the world's most diverting sweet wines.

AUSTRALIA AND NEW ZEALAND

Not many other non-European producers have taken Chenin seriously yet as the base for a varietal wine. There is a tendency to try to make it too rich for its own good by muffling its acidity. Plump, oak-enriched examples crop up in the Swan Valley GI in Western Australia, although the cool climate of New Zealand is a more likely setting for successful Chenin. Some varietal Chenin from the North Island has looked good, but again the tendency is towards a high-extract style.

CALIFORNIA

One or two California wineries have produced convincing varietal dry Chenin, some of it oak-aged. The wines articulate the tart fruit and balancing honey tones of Vouvray, for all that they are appreciably fatter-textured. Otherwise, Chenin goes into everyday blended whites to lend added acidity.

Chenin Blanc, or Steen, vines on the Klein Constantia Estate, South Africa (above). Chenin has been the backbone of the country's white wine production.

Widely spaced Chenin Blanc vines in the Temecula valley, California (left), where the variety is still a minority taste.

VIOGNIER

Viognier's career as an internationally known grape variety has only been very recently established. It is safe to say that, before the early 1990s, the ordinary consumer had probably never heard of it.

THE RISE TO prominence of Viognier over the past decade has been meteoric. Once a niche variety whose name was rarely seen on labels, it is now everywhere, either on its own, or quite often blended in a double-act with Chardonnay. That last detail is a little ironic, as the chief impetus for everybody suddenly deciding to plant the variety was to fulfil the demands of that section of the market that was getting a little tired of subsisting on an unrelieved diet of Chardonnay.

Its spiritual home is in a small appellation at the northern end of the northern sector of the Rhône, called Condrieu. The wines of Condrieu were once one of the wine world's best-kept secrets, and they owed their opulent, perfumed appeal entirely to the Viognier grape. Most often vinified without oak, these are wines that combine the heady, musky scents of ripe orchard fruits (classically apricots) with some powerful spice tones such as cinnamon and cardamom, backed up by big burly texture and high alcohol.

Elsewhere in the region, it is the only permitted grape in the white wines of a micro-appellation within Condrieu, called Château-Grillet, where the wine is made entirely by one producer. It is also, as we saw when discussing Syrah, entitled to form up to 20 per cent of a blend in the red wines of Côte-Rôtie, to which it can contribute an unearthly, often ravishing, layer of floral scent.

When the revolution in French winemaking of the late 1980s established the Languedoc as the nerve-centre of varietal experimentation, Viognier rapidly became one of the favoured grapes of that region. It wasn't that long a journey after all from the northern Rhône, although Vin de Pays d'Oc Viognier is a much simpler and less elegant wine than Condrieu (as well it might be, given the price differential).

As might be guessed from its location in southern France, the variety prefers a fairly warm climate, which is why it has proved particularly suitable for planting in the southern

Viognier (right) has become undoubtedly one of the most fashionable white grape varieties on the international scene, producing aromatic, spicy wines everywhere from the south of France to the hotter regions of Australia.

hemisphere and in the warmer regions of California. The only possible disadvantage to that is that it can lack a little acidity in very warm vintages, which then leaves its fruit flavours tasting slightly mushy. What that in mind, the most conscientious producers pay careful attention to picking times to ensure that the wine retains a freshening lemony streak for balance.

We can perhaps understand why the world was ready for something other than Chardonnay, but why Viognier? The answer to this lies in the immense increase in fashionability that the wines of the Rhône came to enjoy from the 1980s onwards, and which shows no sign of abating. In the northern Rhône especially, Syrah and Viognier played the same pre-eminent role in the vineyards as Cabernet and Chardonnay did elsewhere, and their flavours were seen as usefully distinctive.

Viognier has the structure of the richest Chardonnays, but without needing oak to lend it aromatic personality. It belongs with that category of white wine grapes considered to be naturally aromatic, along with the likes of Gewürztraminer, Riesling and Muscat.

In California, certain quality-conscious producers have achieved results with Viognier that are every bit as gorgeously rich and exotic as the best of Condrieu. There has been a slightly greater tendency to reach for the oak barrel here, but the concentration and extract of the wines is such that they take some judicious wood-ageing in their stride.

The Australians were a little slower off the mark than their American counterparts with Viognier, the variety only starting to become fashionable there in the mid-1990s. Site specification is all. In the hotter districts, the results have been too heavy and clumsy for comfort, but the potential is undoubtedly there, and we can expect to see some more distinguished examples in years to come.

Demand for cuttings of the grape has also rocketed in South America, where both Chile and Argentina are producing convincingly perfumed, unexpectedly subtle Viognier wines with good fruit-acid balance.

FRENCH ORIGINS
Northern Rhône.

WHERE ELSE IS IT GROWN?
Increasingly important in the southern Rhône, Languedoc and Roussillon. Outside Europe, now fashionable in California, Australia, Chile and Argentina.

TASTING NOTES
Its most widely noticed fruit flavour is apricot, which can range from the free-flowing juice and flesh of a fresh ripe Bergeron fruit to the concentrated muskiness of dried Hunzas. Scented white peach may be in there too, and ripe aromatic Comice pear. Supporting that may be subtly delineated spice notes like cardamom, cinnamon or ginger, while the texture of the wine is close-grained and thick like clotted cream. From the hotter regions, it may be distinctly reminiscent of honey-and-lemon throat-soothers.

France

Château-Grillet (above), in its amphitheatre of vines above the river Rhône at Vérin, is one of the smallest appellations in France.

Viognier vines on the Coteau de Vernon (below), from which are made the top wine of Domaine Georges Vernay, long celebrated as one of the most illustrious producers in the whole Condrieu appellation.

The top wines of Condrieu still probably represent the finest expressions of the Viognier grape variety grown anywhere. Other than in the very best Californian examples, it is only really here that the full complexity locked within the grape blossoms forth. For such a small appellation, there is also an intriguing range of styles.

A handful of producers use a touch of oak to round out the texture of the wine and deepen its aromatic impact. It is certainly true that a lick of vanilla, if sensitively applied, can enhance the natural creamy ripeness of the grape in warm vintages, but over-ageing in wood can muddy the waters.

There are also different schools of thought as to how rich and powerful the wine should naturally be, with some preferring an almost delicate, floral style of Condrieu, while others go down the big and blowsy route, emphasizing big alcohol, dense texture and decadently ripe aromas. There are persuasive examples of Viognier in both camps, and indeed it is this very versatility that makes this one of the most fascinating appellations in the whole Rhône valley.

Wholly enclosed with the Condrieu zone is the separate appellation of Château-Grillet which, like certain Burgundy *grands crus*, is exclusively owned by one producer. The style here is quite distinct from Condrieu, with the wine being cask-aged and only released after the next vintage has been made. As a result, the fruit tones are much more muted, leaving just the heftiness of the wine's texture to appreciate.

Many growers in the bulk-producing region of the southern Rhône are now looking to Viognier to add a little aromatic character to their white wines, which have traditionally been rather neutral in flavour. Even so, it is extremely unusual to come across wines that are made from unblended Viognier.

For solo Viognier at kinder prices, it is necessary to head a little further south to the Languedoc, where this grape has become something of a buzz varietal. The wines here don't attempt anything like the complexity of Condrieu, but then the vines themselves are not nearly as ancient. A mouthful of very fresh, apricotty or peachy white, usually unoaked, is to be expected, along with strong alcohol (typically 13.5 per cent), and an often slightly overdone acidic streak with the pronounced flavour of lemon juice. These wines are generally for drinking young, but can benefit from a little ageing to tone down the acidity. They can make a good, if heady, aperitif.

Other Regions

CALIFORNIA

Without a doubt, the best examples of unblended Viognier outside France are being produced in California, specifically in the Napa Valley. Tasted blind, the finest bottlings are all but indistinguishable from best Condrieu, imitating not only the ripe yellow fruits and Indian spices of the Rhône stars, but also their lush, floral, creamy style too. There is also the same debate as to whether oak-ageing suits the wines or not, with exponents of both styles producing some stunning wines. By acclamation, the star winemaker here has been Josh Jensen of Calera, whose small quantities of scintillating wines are as much sought-after (and as hard to find) as the top Condrieus.

At the lower end of the price range, and especially from the northerly Mendocino AVA, there can be a tendency in the wines to that slightly confected honey-and-lemon flavour of proprietary throat-sweets, with all the floral charm and the exotic spice notes missing. However much refined sensibilities may be offended by such tastes, though, these have proved commercially popular wines with the ABC (Anything but Chardonnay) contingent, and plantings of Viognier are on the increase. Quality will undoubtedly continue to improve.

SOUTH AMERICA

Varietal Viogniers from Argentina and Chile have been making their presence felt in the export markets since the late 1990s. The style tends to be big and alcoholic, as elsewhere, but with a little of the honeysuckle charm of Rhône Viognier in the better efforts. Both countries favour an unoaked style over cask-ageing, but with strength prevailing over grace. A strong lemony note underpins the peachy fruit, and the finish may often be quite spirity. Creditable showings have been made by certain of the volume producers in both countries, and we must expect this to be an important varietal in the future.

AUSTRALIA

The honey-and-lemon tendency still vitiates too many of Australia's efforts with Viognier, for all that there are plenty of suitable sites for growing it. Top bottlings can have the structure and intensity as those of the Rhône big boys, but without the aromatic finesse or the subtleties to back them up. The McLaren Vale GI has so far been the most promising stamping-ground.

More eye-catching perhaps than varietal Viognier from Australia has been the practice of adding it to Shiraz to produce a southern-hemisphere homage to those Côte Rôties that have a little Viognier in the blend. There is something peculiar but compelling in finding a waft of clean apricot scent emerging through the inky-dark, blackberry style of strapping Aussie Shiraz. Producers in the Yarra Valley, Victoria, and South Australia's McLaren Vale and Langhorne Creek GIs, have made waves in recent vintages.

Joseph Phelps Vineyards (above), at St Helena, in Napa County, California, has been among the trailblazers for varietal Viognier in what many now regard as its second home after the Rhône.

A gum tree in the Heggies vineyard of Yalumba (left), in the Eden Valley, South Australia. Viogniers from regions as hot as this usually have the structure and alcohol levels of certain Rhône examples, though perhaps don't always have the same aromatic finesse.

GEWURZTRAMINER

Unique among the white varieties, Gewürztraminer is very much a love-it-or-hate-it grape. Once tasted, never forgotten, its ostentatious, scented, rich character has made it the grape forever associated with Alsace.

WHETHER OR NOT you enjoyed it, your first taste of Gewürztraminer is likely to have made an impression. While a simple Chardonnay may seem shy and retiring in the glass, Gewürz comes screaming out at you with some of the most unearthly and downright bizarre scents and flavours to be found anywhere in the world of wine. So strange can it taste that those encountering it unexpectedly for the first time may wonder whether it has had some other flavouring added to it.

The parent variety seems to be of north Italian extraction, in a grape known simply as Traminer. Its highly scented offshoot, first identified in the 19th century, took its prefix from the German word for 'spice'. By this time, the grape had acquired, by natural mutation, a deep pink skin in place of the green one, and had begun to yield an extraordinarily perfumed juice. Popular in Germany, Gewürz was widely planted in Alsace during the period of the region's absorption into Germany in the late 19th century.

Alsace, now incontrovertibly French, is the variety's first home today. While there are increasingly impressive examples being produced elsewhere, particularly in Germany, they never quite seem to attain the uninhibited aromatic splendour of the greatest Alsace Gewürz. In an especially ripe year, it may combine musky fruit notes like lychee and squishy apricot, with ginger, cloves, talcum powder, and a whole florist's shop of roses, violets and jasmine. It is usually pretty low in acidity, which makes it drinkable quite young, but roaring with alcohol, so that a little – combined with those unsubtle flavours – goes an exhaustingly long way.

Because of its larger-than-life character, Gewürz is constantly in danger of not being taken terribly seriously by those who are used to more restrained flavours in a white wine. In the long dry summers of Alsace, it ripens to a tremendous richness, which accounts for all that alcohol, but even when fermented up to around the 14–15 per cent levels I have seen on some, it still seems to retain a core of residual sugar that leads a lot of consumers to find it too sweet for a supposedly dry wine.

Once the taste is acquired, however, it becomes clear that Gewürztraminer is without doubt one of the classic wine grapes. From a *grand cru* vineyard site owned by one of the top producers in Alsace, its peculiar intensity can be a mightily refreshing antidote to the containerloads of tell-em-apart Chardonnay that the wine market is still awash with. The best Gewürzes will age, although they tend to be the ones that have unusually pronounced acidity to begin with, and there are not too many of these. You can bump up acid levels by picking the grapes earlier, but then you risk losing some of that striking flavour.

The dilemma over picking times is problem enough in Alsace. In warmer climates, it becomes a complete headache. The difficulties of timing it right account for why most efforts outside Alsace have so far failed to match the quality of the best wines produced in this one enclave of northeastern France. That said, some German growers are beginning to achieve convincing results with the variety, especially in the slightly warmer areas of the Pfalz and Baden. New Zealand is giving it its best shot, and there are isolated stars in Chile and the United States. One or two South African examples have been particularly exciting.

For a grape that seems to be telling the winemaker that it wants to be sweet, it comes as no surprise to find that many Alsace and German growers make a late-picked Gewürz in the form of flowery Spätlese and Auslese in Germany, and peach-scented Vendange Tardive in Alsace. When conditions are right, the grape can acquire botrytis, and a fully rotted wine is labelled Sélection de Grains Nobles in Alsace. These are massively dense, opulent dessert wines, tasting like orange and ginger marmalade – one of the great taste experiences. They can age for many years in the bottle.

The unmistakable livery of the Gewürztraminer grape (right). Unlike the green or golden colour of its fellow white grapes, Gewürz sports a dusky pink skin – a fitting outer expression of its flowery, highly perfumed character.

ORIGINS

For the Gewürztraminer specifically, possibly Alsace. For its less intoxicatingly scented forebear, Traminer, probably the south Tyrol area of northern Italy.

WHERE ELSE IS IT GROWN?

Apart from Alsace, it has important bases in Germany and Austria, less so in Spain and eastern Europe. Experimental plantings dotted around the southern hemisphere, and also the United States, particularly the Pacific Northwest.

TASTING NOTES

The list is well-nigh endless. Fruits are usually an eerily precise imitation of ripely juicy lychees, together with overripe peach or nectarine when the flesh is just starting to turn mushy. Some authorities dispute the spice connection evoked in the German word *Gewürz*, but there is nearly always a good sprinkling of ground ginger and often cinnamon, occasionally the scent of whole cloves and even a dusting of white pepper. Flowers are very much in evidence too – violets and rose-petals (often reminiscent of attar of roses, as in Turkish Delight) – and then there is a whole range of scented bathroom products – aromatic bath salts, perfumed soap, talcum powder. Gewürz from regions other than Alsace may present a toned-down version of all that, which may come as a relief to some.

Alsace

Gewurztraminer (spelt without the *umlaut* in France) accounts for just under a fifth of total vineyard plantings in Alsace. It is one of the favoured grapes permitted in the designated *grand cru* areas. Although Riesling is unofficially thought of as the first among this top division by the growers themselves, Gewurz is cherished for the forthright character that has made it the grape most ineradicably associated in consumers' minds with the region as a whole. Blowsy, spicy, exotic Gewurz just is the taste of Alsace.

The grape does exceptionally well on the often rather claggy clay-based soils found in the Haut-Rhin area of Alsace. Its willingness to ripen well in the generally dry vintages of this very sheltered region allows its personality to shine through in the finished wine. In many ways, it is the antithesis in Alsace of the Riesling we looked at earlier, giving more alcohol and less acidity, resulting in a considerably more forward style of wine.

Another quality that marks Gewurz wines out from their counterparts is their very deep

The Clos Windsbuhl vineyard at Hunawihr, owned by Zind-Humbrecht (below). The Gewurztraminer from this site is one of the finest examples of what Alsace Gewurz can achieve.

colour. They usually have a richly burnished golden tone, not dissimilar to the most heavily oaked Chardonnays, a characteristic derived in Gewurz's case not from wooden barrels but from the distinctive pigmentation of the grapeskin. Whereas most white varieties come in conventional shades of green, Gewurz, as befits its gaudy nature, is turned out in a deep pink livery that lends some of its blush to the wine itself, very occasionally showing even as a faint pinkish tinge behind the deep yellow.

In the cooler years in Alsace, Gewurztraminer can seem a rather pale imitation of itself, both in terms of colour and flavours. The vintage of 2001 wasn't particularly good, for example, and the wines' resulting balance was seriously skewed, leaving an overall impression of weight, but without the depth of flavour to carry it off with any grace.

The classification of the *grand cru* sites came into effect in Alsace in the 1980s. While dogged inevitably by controversy over what should be included and what not, it has since emerged

that much of the land that has been incorporated is of sufficient quality to inspire the producers to their greatest efforts. Of the 51 sites, some of the best for Gewurztraminer are Brand, Goldert, Hengst, Kessler, Sporen, Steinert and Zotzenberg, but there are many more.

Wines with those names on the label are undoubtedly worth the extra cost over a bottle of everyday Gewurz. Many producers are in the habit of labelling their wines Cuvée Réserve or something similar, supposedly indicating notably successful batches of a particular vintage, but these terms, unlike *grand cru*, have no legal force.

What is probably more important than anything pertaining to labelling in Alsace is the grape yields. Almost without exception, the best wines, whatever their designation, are sourced from older, lower-yielding vines. Much more

than about 50 hectolitres per hectare, and you're liable to produce a wine that lacks true focus, while some of the finest wines are being vinified off barely more than 25 hl/ha. It may cost twice as much, but then you're buying twice the concentration, and concentrated flavours are what Alsace is all about.

Cooperatives are an important part of the wine scene in Alsace, and vary enormously in quality, but one of the most commercially significant, exporting substantial quantities – the Caves de Turckheim – is one of the most reliable. At the stratospheric end of the spectrum, wines from some of the old-established family vineyards, particularly some of the Vendange Tardive bottlings from *grand cru* sites like Hengst and Goldert, are unutterably exquisite, powerful essences of this most ostentatious grape.

Gewurztraminer grapes left on the vine until November (above), destined for the peach-scented style of Alsace Vendange Tardive.

Other Regions

GERMANY
Although plantings of Gewürztraminer in Germany are by no means extensive, some German growers have achieved notable successes with it in the light-textured, low-alcohol styles for which the country is renowned. It fares better in the warmer regions such as Baden in the south, and the Pfalz, where its best manifestations are brimful of expressive ripe fruit.

UNITED STATES
As others of the Alsace grapes, such as Riesling and Pinot Gris, have thrived in the states of the Pacific Northwest, so Gewürz has also done its bit. Success has come patchily, and the results are not as yet much exported. There are some reasonably tasty examples in Washington State, including a handful of delicate but attractive late-harvest versions.

NEW ZEALAND AND AUSTRALIA
The cooler climate of New Zealand is better for Gewürz than most of Australia (where the grape has often been used simply as blending material for dry Riesling). The North Island regions of Gisborne and Auckland, as well as Central Otago on the South Island, have produced some convincing attempts, but the weight is often lacking, and the perfume more fugitive.

ELSEWHERE
The occasional quietly impressive Gewürz does crop up in other countries, for all that we don't really want Gewürz to be quiet. Chile has some properly scented wines, and one or two South African growers are getting the hang of it rather impressively. It has proved to be a useful blender with Muscat in Penedés in northeastern Spain, especially from Torres.

Matua Valley Winery, set amid its vineyards in the Auckland area of New Zealand's North Island (above). Matua Valley is one of New Zealand's most notable producers of characterful Gewürztraminer.

GAMAY

The one classic grape variety that has stayed close to home, Gamay is synonymous with Beaujolais, that light, fresh, strawberry-fruity red that is mostly designed to be drunk young and lively, but whose best wines will age.

LOOKING AT a map of the world distribution of grape varieties might seem to suggest that Gamay is something of an interloper among our exalted company of 12 noble grapes. A red blob shows a significant concentration of it in eastern France, with only the skimpiest of traces anywhere else. In fact, it gets in because that red blob constitutes one of the world's most individualistic red wine styles – Beaujolais.

Gamay is the only grape used in the making of (red) Beaujolais. Some of it is also grown further north, in the southern stretch of Burgundy known as the Mâconnais, where it's responsible for usually rather indifferent wines bottled as Mâcon Rouge. Elsewhere, it may be blended in a proportion of up to two-thirds with Pinot Noir to make Bourgogne Passetoutgrains. A fair bit is grown in the Loire valley to the west, some as Touraine Gamay, some used in Crémant de Loire pink fizz. On the western flank of the central Rhône, in the Coteaux de l'Ardèche, it makes spicy reds to rival the Grenache-based wines of Côtes du Rhône.

It is on the stern granite hillsides of Beaujolais, however, that Gamay really comes into its own. In addition to basic Beaujolais and Beaujolais-Villages, there are ten villages that are theoretically capable of making the best wine (known as *cru* Beaujolais), and which have their their own appellations within the region. Running north to south, these are: St-Amour, Juliénas, Chénas, Moulin-à-Vent, Fleurie, Chiroubles, Morgon, Régnié, Brouilly and Côte de Brouilly. The last is a peculiar little hill of blue granite that pops up in the middle of the larger Brouilly appellation.

There are some subtle stylistic differences among these ten, but what links them is more important than what distinguishes them, and that is the sunny-natured Gamay grape. Gamay offers the lightest possible style of red wine, full of simple strawberry fruit, fresh sappy acids,

and little or no tannin. Although the best growers do achieve a certain measure of complexity in their wines, and some of the best *cru* Beaujolais can age well for five or six years, most producers are content to turn out oceans of straightforward quaffing wine that reacts appetizingly to chilling for summer drinking.

The light texture of Beaujolais derives from a method of vinification called carbonic maceration, to which Gamay is especially suited. Instead of being crushed in the normal way, which extracts some tannin from the skins and pips along with the juice, the grapes are tipped whole into fermenters from which the air has been driven out with carbon dioxide. The juice starts to ferment inside the whole grapes, until the skins burst from the build-up of gas within them. The grapes at the bottom of the heap are punctured by the weight of those on top, and ferment in the normal way, but that is still gentler than most assisted forms of pressing.

Gamay's suitability for producing cheap, early-drinking, featherweight reds is what inspired the marketing of Beaujolais Nouveau, which continues to this day. Those who feel like imbibing quantities of embryonic, just-fermented, acid-tingling red from the very latest vintage can indulge their passion freely in the third week of November.

There is a movement afoot in the region to introduce greater depth into the wines in an attempt to throw the happy-go-lucky, knock-it-back image of Beaujolais into some sort of relief. Some are using a proportion of normally fermented juice in order to inject a little tannic kick; others are ageing in new oak barrels in a region where such a thing was once anathema. Such courageous swimming against the tide has resulted in top *cuvées* of *cru* Beaujolais that have the gingery, brambly concentration of northern Rhône Syrah (no, really).

External markets are still dominated by the wines of the powerful bulk producer Georges Duboeuf. For once, quantity does not preclude quality because most of the company's wines are good, and easily recognizable by their distinctive flower labels.

Gamay (right) offers the lightest style of red wine, full of simple strawberry fruit, fresh, sappy acids and very little tannin.

About 10 per cent of the vineyard land in Switzerland is planted with Gamay, where it is often blended with the far more widely grown Pinot Noir, and there are one or two producers in California doing their best with it, and achieving reasonable approximations of the style of young *cru* Beaujolais.

By and large, however, Gamay hasn't performed well on soils different to those of its native region. Coupled with the fact that the style of wine it is happiest producing has not been a noticeably fashionable one for red wines in recent years, there isn't the incentive that there is with a variety like Pinot Noir to compete with the best of France. All of which is a shame because, when on song, Gamay is among the most effortlessly charming styles of young red wine. (Its rosés, by contrast, are probably best passed over in silence.)

Misty autumnal scene in Brouilly (left), one of the ten crus *of the Beaujolais region.*

FRENCH ORIGINS
Beaujolais.

WHERE ELSE IS IT GROWN?
Burgundy, Loire, Rhône. Switzerland and other central European countries. Minute amounts in California.

TASTING NOTES
At its deliriously ripest, fistfuls of pulpy wild strawberries. When very young (as Nouveau, particularly) it can have a synthetic smell like boiled sweets, reinforced by the crunchiness of its acidity in the mouth. That, and related aromas like peardrops (pear candy), banana flavouring and bubblegum, are all fermentation smells accentuated by the fact that no air gets into it while it is vinifying. Some of the richer, meatier *cru* wines can take on the attributes of mature Pinot Noir after five or six years.

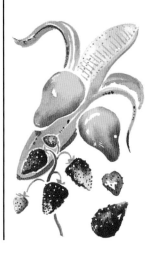

INDEX